TWICE AROUND THE BAY

Christina Hall

ISIS
LARGE PRINT
Oxford

First published in Great Britain 2001
by
Birlinn Limited

Published in Large Print 2008 by ISIS Publishing Ltd.,
7 Centremead, Osney Mead, Oxford OX2 0ES
by arrangement with
Birlinn Limited

British Library Cataloguing in Publication Data
Hall, Christina
    Twice around the bay. – Large print ed.
    (Isis reminiscence series)
    1. Hall, Christina – Childhood and youth
    2. Hall, Christina – Homes and haunts – Scotland
    – South Uist
    3. Large type books
    4. South Uist (Scotland) – Social life and
    customs – 20th century
    I. Title
    941.1'4084'092

ISBN 978–0–7531–9514–7 (hb)
ISBN 978–0–7531–9515–4 (pb)

Printed and bound in Great Britain by
T. J. International Ltd., Padstow, Cornwall

For Norman, Philip and Shona

Uibhist nam Beanntan

Air an fhonn *An t-Eilean Dorcha*

Nuair bhios mi leam fhìn
Agus m' inntinn fo leòn,
Bidh mi cuimhneachadh uair
'S mi gun uallach 's gun bhròn,
'S mi a' ruith is a' ruaig
Feadh nam bruachan 's nan lòn
Gu làithean m' oig'
Ann an Uibhist nam beanntan.

Fonn

'S ann gun strì rachainn sìos
Air dhà sgiathaidh mo smuain
Gu tràigh mhòr an taobh 'n iar,
'G èisteachd fìor-ghlag a' chuain;
A' ghainmheach gheal mhìn
'S i gu h-ìseal fom bhonn,
Is gach tonn a' seinn
"Uibhist nam Beanntan".

Anns a' mhadainn gum b' èibhinn
Leam èirigh moch tràth
Is an driùchd air gach gèig —
Bidh an sprèidh len cuid àil,
Is an uiseag bheag bhinn-ghuthach
Dìreadh gu h-àrd

A' cur fàilte
Air Uibhist nam beanntan.

Ged a tha mise 'n-dràst'
Ann am baile na strì,
'S mi cho fada bhon àit'
Anns na dh'àraicheadh mi,
Gu bheil sàsachadh àraidh
Toirt blàths do mo chrìdh —
'S e gun till mi
Gu Uibhist nam beanntan.

Donald John MacMillan
London, 1965

Uist of Mountains

Tune: *The Dark Island*

When I'm all on my own,
Feeling mournful in mind,
Carefree days of my childhood
In my memory I find:
I run over the fields
Where the brown streams unwind
To my young days
In Uist of mountains.

Chorus:

Then with ease on the wings
Of my memory I soar,
The Atlantic before me
A welcoming roar;
Barefoot running through
Silvery sands on the shore,
As each wave sings out,
"Uist of Mountains".

At the dawn to awake
With the dew on the ground,
When the cattle start moving,
Calves calling for cows
High above me the skylark's
Sweet voice would pronounce

Salutations for
Uist of mountains.

Though I'm far from the birthplace
That nurtured my soul,
And the strain of the city
Is taking its toll,
I'm sustained by the hope
That one day I will go
Back to my home
In Uist of mountains.

English version: Alick MacMillan
Glasgow 1999

CHAPTER
ONE

"Wake up! Wake up! If you're not on the bus in ten minutes you're walking it!"

I was catapulted from my deep sleep, the kind of near-death stupor which follows a night spent dancing Highland reels and falling into bed at dawn with my fingers in my ears to block out the noise of birdsong. As I struggled to focus my eyes on the bedroom door, I could not believe the face I saw there.

"OK! Just go away, five minutes will do me . . . I promise!"

As the door closed I was already jumping into my clothes and gathering my school books. My father and brother had long gone to work and I could dimly remember my mother giving me a wake-up call before going down to the far end of the croft to milk the cows. Obviously it hadn't worked, and although my mind had gone through the motions of getting up and dressing, my body had stayed in bed. My second and final warning had come from Fergus the driver of the school bus, and the reason I found this so embarrassing was that I was not one of his pupil passengers — I was the teacher.

By the early 1960s the houses on the Hebridean island of South Uist were all much of a muchness; a few thatched houses remained but most of them had been replaced by two types of bungalow. Also scattered around were the strong, stone-built, two-storied houses which gave testimony to ancestral affluence and can still be seen on the island. The layout of living areas and bedrooms was the same in most of the new houses like ours and so, having waited outside the gate for some time, Fergus had come in and searched until he found me and delivered his ultimatum. It is the kind of awakening which only happened once in my lifetime and one I will never forget.

I was back! Back on the island where north is down and south is up, where the only reliable weather forecast comes from looking out of the window. South Uist, the place where I was born and where I had spent only seven and a half consecutive years in our little thatched house with my lovely if sometimes chaotic family throughout my whole childhood.

I had been raised on Benbecula and Barra by a teacher aunt and her housekeeping sister, and my school-holiday visits home had been precious and had kept me going throughout what was a fairly strict and lonely time. Then came the three years at Daliburgh School, when I found that being back with the family was something which took a bit of getting used to, and by the time I had settled in it was time to leave for Fort William and senior secondary school, followed by three more years in exile at Notre Dame College of Education in Glasgow, all to fulfil my ambition of

2

becoming a teacher in an island school. Now, as they say in the Bible, it had come to pass.

South Uist lies due west of the Isle of Skye and is part of the long string of islands joined together by causeways and known as the Outer Hebrides. Today time has moved on and it is a place where progress and tradition live in harmony. The modernisation of the island and its inhabitants, which began at the end of the war, came slowly at first but soon gathered momentum, and when I returned I found that much had changed since I had left the island to complete my education. But there was still a long way to go to reach the islanders' present living conditions.

Ambition is not a characteristic with which writers over the years have credited Hebrideans. In fact, the inhabitants of my own island were once slanderously described as work-shy and unintelligent by a certain renowned author, not one of my favourite people. We may not be as forceful and brash about achieving our aims as your average Lowlander but, believe me, we know ambition. I had decided that I was going to be a teacher very early in life — well, perhaps not, it was more a case of deciding to be a student, and I had worked hard and endured much in order to achieve this and make it work.

My academic ability was a good average but nothing special; in the more relaxed atmosphere of a college campus I saw many students fall by the wayside, and it would have been so easy to do likewise. However, I managed to enjoy every minute of my free time and ensure that the coursework got done as necessary. No matter how much time I spent away from home, letters from my parents and the college holidays kept the island at the forefront of my mind, and it was a proud day indeed when I received a letter from J. A. MacLean, Director of Education for Inverness-shire, informing me that I had been appointed as Teacher-in-Charge of South Glendale Primary School, South Uist.

In those far-off days when a crofter's family was a tight unit and children were considered a valuable commodity to be nurtured by their parents, talked to and guided by their elders, there were often three generations of the same family in the village, if not still sharing a home. Television and computers had not yet taken the place of family conversation, and old people who were respected as having a valid place in island society passed much folklore and wisdom down the ladder of years.

This child-nurturing philosophy meant that no matter how isolated a community was, there was a primary school within walking distance from the child's home. Sometimes the entire roll would be in single figures, but the formal school building and the provision of books and teacher gave the children the same chance of an education as their peers in much larger communities, without their having to leave home at a very early hour and be transported to a large central school. Small rural primary schools abounded in the Highlands and Islands at that time; such a school was South Glendale.

Nowadays getting to South Glendale is easy — you get into your car and drive there. In the days when I was appointed as teacher it wasn't so simple, as the village was inaccessible by road. The bus driver who woke me up was doing me a great favour by transporting me part of the way. He was passing our house with an empty bus on his way to Ludag to pick up children from the south end of the island and bring them to Daliburgh Junior Secondary School.

Under strict instructions from his employers not to pick anyone else up, he was really risking his job by doing me this favour, but that's Uist folk for you: I never had to walk to Ludag, even if the noise of the bus's horn being leaned on, as Fergus got tired of waiting outside our house, sometimes frightened the cows.

Ludag was the end of the road. Literally. The spine road, which ran the whole length of the island, came to its southernmost conclusion at Polachar Inn and another long spur veered off eastwards towards Ludag jetty. I had never even seen South Glendale and was very excited at the thought of teaching there. I had visions of living at home and travelling to the school every day, but when I first went out to see the place I found that this was simply impossible. The only vehicle our household could boast, apart from a small tractor, was an equally small motorbike, and this was how I went to take my first look at the terrain, on the pillion of a little "putt-putt" ridden by my father.

"The only way to climb that hill is by boat!" On Ludag jetty we had been joined by Neil Campbell, the ferryman, who had spent most of his adult life on the water, and despite the twinkle in his eye, which betrayed the fact that this was not the first time he had used that line, I had to agree with him. Between my first school and me rose a rugged expanse of heather-clad hill. There was a well-worn track meandering around the base, gradually increasing in gradient until it disappeared into the horizon about halfway up the hill. The sea lapped around the rocks and clumps of heather at the base of the hill and surged on around it and out of our field of vision, where it curved inwards to form a bay. Round this bay stood the tiny village of South Glendale with its little corrugated-iron school. Things did not look good and I could see my social life vanishing before my very eyes.

Sailing cost money and I had none. My monthly salary would be £36 clear, inclusive of Isolation Grant and Responsibility Allowance, and although this was higher than my father's monthly salary from Alginate Industries, I had to work for a month before receiving it: so the hill it had to be. With a sinking heart I contemplated my varnished toenails peeping out of fashionable sandals and remembered another fact of island life — the Wellington boot will become an essential part of your wardrobe regardless of your age, sex or professional status.

"How long will it take me to get there?" I asked Neil, anxiously.

"On a day like this with a moderate wind, I'd say the back of half an hour." Then he added, "If there's a gale behind you and you lift your feet, you could be there in ten minutes. On the other hand, if you couldn't stop running you could end up missing it altogether."

Both he and my father thought that this was very funny and walked off chuckling.

Neil has often been mentioned in books about the island, in particular by writers who have used his services as ferryman over the years as a way of visiting other islands. Tall and well-built, with permanently tanned features, he had the quiet calm bearing of a man who knew exactly why he had been put on this earth. The sea was his workplace and before the arrival of the present day multi-million pound car ferry and causeway link to Eriskay he would transport people over there, or further on to Barra, in his boat.

No matter what the weather threw at him, and although the boat was open and powered only by a small engine, if you wanted to cross the *Caolas* (Sound), Neil was your man. He regarded the sea with a respect which held no trace of fear. He also regarded the Glendale teachers as beings who had been put on this earth to amaze and amuse him in fairly equal quantities, and who could blame him?

The teachers assigned to the little isolated school were always female and nearly always new to the profession. They were young, idealistic graduates of a college of education where teaching was regarded as a sacred vocation and the words "I am a career teacher" would have earned them instant expulsion, if not excommunication.

True, they would have cut their teaching teeth on the children of Glasgow while at college. If my own personal experience is anything to go by, students doing teaching practice were often used as unpaid supply teachers and could be stuck in front of forty Gorbals street-war veterans for a week before they had time to say, "I am only allowed to teach one unsupervised lesson." It was a very valuable part of training but a million miles from the Glendale scenario. That thought crossed my mind as I looked across the Sound of Eriskay and knew that I would be seeing a lot more of it in days to come.

Although South Glendale and the hill were foreign territory to me, I was quite familiar with Ludag. I had been there many times before, as a young girl on my way to the island of Eriskay to spend the weekend with a friend from Daliburgh School, a girl called Margaret who boarded with relatives near my home. Her mother knew mine and Margaret came to our house from time to time. It was always a hospitable house and, though small, thatched and crowded with MacMillans, she always enjoyed visiting us. In return she would invite me to go with her at weekends to the tiny island which was her home.

We would go up to Ludag on the school bus on a Friday afternoon and Neil Campbell would ferry us across the Sound along with the other Eriskay people who had come over to Uist for a dental appointment or a shopping trip or whatever. We would come back on the Sunday evening, and as there was no bus service at the weekends, we would walk home. Distance seemed to matter not a bit. Feet were there for using. Having spent so many years under virtual house arrest living with my aunts, I can't begin to describe the joy of being able to go off to another island with a friend and my parents' blessing.

The little island of Eriskay has been immortalised in the hauntingly beautiful "Eriskay Love Lilt" collected and made popular by Marjorie Kennedy Fraser. It is the subject of many books and photographic works: *Father Allan's Island, Eriskay, a Poem of Remote Lives*, and the recent *Eriskay Where I Was Born* by Angus Edward MacInnes, to mention but a few. It measures two and a half miles from north to south and is less than two miles wide. An old friend of my Glendale teaching days once told me, "When the good Lord finished making Uist, he found a bit of specially blessed earth under his nails. He scraped it out and flicked it into the Sound and the next day there was Eriskay."

The truth is not quite as romantic. Gordon of Cluny acquired the island in 1838 and used it as a dumping-ground for the victims of his infamous Clearances. Although the soil was poor and rocky, the hardy islanders knew that they had two choices — survive by whatever means they could, or die. In unimaginable circumstances they made that barren, rocky, wind-lashed scrap of an island, and the sea around it, support themselves and future generations.

I recently read a book written by an American who had come to the Hebrides to trace his ancestors. Of the Clearances he writes: "The crofters were given a choice of moving nearer the sea or emigrating. As most of them disliked the sea, they decided to take the softer option of assisted emigration."

No comment. Who has not heard of people driven off their land to Badbea in Helmsdale to make room for sheep who had to tie their children and cattle to posts to prevent them being blown over the cliffs? When the harvest was poor and they could not pay the rent for their pitiful bits of land, the landowners burned their houses and drove them on to the emigration ships.

The Eriskay settlers had been "cleared" at least twice before being sent to Eriskay. Then there were the Barra crofters of 1851. The 1500 crofters to whom I refer thought that they were going to a meeting to discuss rents. Instead they found themselves brutalised and bound between the stinking decks of wooden ships on their way to America — if, that is, they survived the cholera. Soft option? Assisted emigration? Yeah, right!

Despite the gruelling hardship which was the pattern of their daily lives, the people of Eriskay survived and at the time of my visits the population was about 200 people. This may seem tiny as head counts go, and it was not the least populated Hebridean island of the time. Berneray had even fewer people and the least populated was Vatersay, with less than 100 inhabitants.

Perhaps the most famous visitor Eriskay ever had was Bonnie Prince Charlie, who landed there on 23 July 1745, when he sailed over from France at the start of his attempt to reclaim Scotland for the Stuarts. He sheltered in a cove which is named Coilleag a' Phrionnsa (the Prince's Dell), and there he is reputed to have planted a species of convolvulus called Flùr a'

Phrionnsa (the Prince's Flower). We saw the flowers, Margaret and I, and the little hollow in which they grew looked just the right shape for a weary traveller to rest: a splash of soft colour against the bleak landscape, as out of place as the pretty Prince must have felt, standing on the shores of Eriskay. Had he been able to look into the future and see the terrible price his loyal followers would have to pay for rising to his cause, he might have heeded MacDonald of Boisdale's advice and gone straight back to France.

Margaret's family lived in a house with a thatched roof much like our own in our Daliburgh schooldays, and they were kind and welcoming. We talked a lot. Margaret's mother seemed to know everybody who lived in South Uist and we spent a lot of time bringing her up to date on births, marriages and deaths. In return she gave us nuggets of information which often surprised us about some of the more prominent islanders, always starting off by saying, "I shouldn't tell you this, but . . ."

On Saturdays we went to the shop and helped around the croft. As there were no men in the house, I could find myself holding a fence post while Margaret's sister hammered it into the ground, and doing other jobs which were done at home by my father and brothers — it was not very exciting but it was different. Eriskay women were very self-reliant and equal to any chore, as they spent much time holding the croft together while the menfolk were at sea.

In the evenings Morag, Margaret's older sister, any visitors and Margaret and I played cards, while her mother knitted the most wonderfully intricate patterns into fishermen's jerseys for her husband and son. I have heard it said that in a seafaring community like Eriskay each wife had her own individual patterns, which she knitted into the hardwearing socks and jerseys that all the sailors wore. The patterns, handed down through the generations, were as individual as a signature or indeed a fingerprint.

The wool was oiled and could withstand both wind and salty sea spray, so that, in common with the jerseys worn by the Guernsey fishermen, the Eriskay patterns could serve as a means of identification when time spent in the sea rendered a drowned sailor's body unrecognisable.

Like a vast percentage of Eriskay men and men from other islands, Margaret's father and brother were both deep-sea sailors. This was the term used to distinguish men who went to the mainland ports and picked up berths on merchant navy vessels bound for destinations all over the world from others who only sailed in British waters. The island sailing men were always in demand, as they were hardworking and reliable, often working their way up to positions of authority. Other sailors went to South Georgia and lived there for six months, working either on the "catcher" — the ship that chased and caught the whales — or on the factory ship where the dead mammals were processed.

The South Georgia men lived a fairly monastic life, as it was a work-eat-sleep environment, but they came home with huge amounts of money, having had no opportunity to spend it for six months. As my brother said in his song *Tioram air Tir* ("The Whaler's Lament") "*an t-airgead ga chosnadh, 's gun dòigh air chur bhuainn, 's e sìor losgadh toll 'na mo phòcaid*" ("piled up money, with no place to spend it, setting my pocket on fire").

At the end of their long voyages the deep-sea sailors would come home with tales of wondrous things that they had seen on their travels and many souvenirs of foreign lands. Strange carved figures, paper-thin Japanese tea-sets with a Geisha girl's head hidden in the bases of the cups, trays inlaid with butterfly wings and suchlike exotica were often to be seen in the crofthouses of deep-sea sailors.

During the post-war rationing period the sailors' double-ration entitlement enabled them to come home with huge tins of jam, big bags of sugar, large tins of Capstan and Senior Service cigarettes and many other luxury goods in short supply on the island. The money they brought back was a lifeline to their families and it meant that they themselves could spend a few months back on dry land before the call of the sailor's life beckoned them again.

They did not all return. Long periods of abstinence followed by mammoth binges when the ship was in a foreign port sometimes had heartbreaking consequences, and I know of one young man who went out celebrating the end of a long voyage, drinking the night away with his friends in some dockside bar on the other side of the world. Not too steady on his feet as he made his way up the steep gangplank, he stumbled and fell backwards on to the concrete dock. He never got up again.

At least one other contemporary of mine "jumped ship", in Tasmania. It was almost impossible to come back to this country if you had done this, and he is still over there. I saw him on Gaelic TV recently and he has made a good life for himself, but I remember his mother talking to mine and crying her heart out more than once. The sailors were not the only ones who had a hard time.

As we sat in Margaret's house playing "Catch The Ten" and "Old Maid", by the hissing light of the Tilley lamp, we listened to the radio. Reception was crackly on the old battery and accumulator wireless, and no matter how many knobs you turned and tuned, an Italian station kept breaking in. One night Margaret's mother got fed up with all the fiddling and changes of music and language and, getting up, threw her knitting to one side and tuned the radio straight into the middle of the Italian signal, shouting, "*Mura faigh sibh Radio Luxembourg, gabhaibh ur diol de Radio Mussolini! Tha mo cheann-sa gu sgàineadh!*" ("If you can't get Radio Luxembourg, you can have your fill of Radio Mussolini, my head is splitting").

So every time I visited we played cards to "Radio Mussolini". The voices of Italian tenors seemed to blend in quite well with the background sounds of wind and sea from outside.

I have great memories of that little house in Eriskay. To me its inhabitants epitomised many of the complex and fascinating mixture of qualities that made the first settlers on the island determined to survive against all odds. I can still picture Margaret's mother standing in her little kitchen in front of a big black stove making our dinner, a small rotund lady of late middle years, her face sweetly featured but deeply lined and burnt brown by sun and wind. Hanging to her waist was a thick plait of equally mixed brown and grey hair that she rolled into a bun when she went "out on the town", as she called her shopping or church trips. In my memory she is wearing the flowered overall that in the days of my youth appeared to be the garment that you changed into when you took your wedding dress off. On her feet are the Wellington boots necessary for so many outside chores in an all-female household that taking them off was a waste of time.

"*A Dhia Fhlathanais, cuiridh am buntàta uaine seo a' bhuinneach oirnn ach chan eil an còrr againn — fàgaidh e làn sinn airson greis*" ("God in Heaven, these green potatoes will give us the runs, but they're all we have. They'll fill us for a while anyway").

As she scraped away at the blighted potatoes and fried them with *cudaigean* (young saithe or coalfish), she entertained us with such a tuneful and soulful version of "O Sole Mio", picked up from Radio Mussolini that it would have put Pavarotti to shame.

I have seen very little of Margaret and even less of her family since our days at Daliburgh Junior Secondary School, but I have thought of her many a time. I remember her and her family and our days on Eriskay, before the car ferry made it easy for the tourists to visit it and the young folk to leave it. I

15

thought of her as I walked over the hill and round the coast to my little school in South Glendale, on days when the early morning mist hung low over the Sound and Eriskay in the near distance appeared to be suspended in mid-air above a sea so glittery and blue that it hurt my eyes.

I walked the hill and sometimes ran it, as Neil had forecast, every Friday after school and Monday mornings to get back to my lodgings, the house where all the teachers over the years had been well looked after by the MacIntyre family. Often the lure of a dance, concert or a boyfriend would make the walk seem less arduous and I would go home mid-week as well. The best dances were always the furthest away, and sometimes I only got back home to bed at six in the morning. All things considered, despite the hill walking, I had reason to be grateful that my post was not as demanding as working in a city school and that the bus driver was a saint.

CHAPTER
TWO

I had abandoned the idea of living at home and had arranged to board in Glendale during the week, coming home at weekends, and when I went out to South Glendale to take up my lodgings my mother went with me. I had made a couple of half-day visits to the school to familiarise myself with the building and the children's records, as you do, and each time I seemed to lose the path on the return journey — no sense of direction, not then, not now.

My mother was worried about me and wanted to make sure that I was going to find the place and be all right out there. We had contacted my future landlady by phone and had agreed that my mother could stay with me for the night, and we travelled to Ludag on the mail-boat bus which ran from Lochboisdale three days a week. She arranged to get a lift back the next morning on the school bus. As the boat came in at about 7p.m., and by the time the passengers had boarded the bus and it had travelled through the townships to Ludag, stopping here and there, we knew that it would be late before we arrived at our destination and set off across the hill. It was a dark lowering kind of evening, so we thought we'd better take a torch.

Things went well for part of the way, and although we were well burdened with my luggage, we would have made good time if we hadn't followed a sheep-track for about fifteen minutes until we realised that we were getting nowhere fast. By the time we got back on to the proper track it was really dark and we had to keep our eyes firmly on the ground, as we didn't want to be misled into taking another detour. I noticed that my mother kept looking over her shoulder, but as my mind was busy going over the things I would have to do on my first day and hadn't noticed anything out of the ordinary in our surroundings, I didn't say anything to her.

After a while, when I began to puff a little, I realised that she had stepped up the pace considerably and that we were practically running, so I asked her if anything was wrong. "Listen," she said, stopping and pointing in the direction from which we had come. I could hear ghostly voices and strange laughter carried on the now brisk wind, and the eerie sounds made the hairs on the back of my neck stand up. Fortunately, by this time we could see the lights from the Glendale houses and we walked very fast, keeping as close to each other as we could. The house we were aiming for was the first in the village and we nearly ran through the door when it was opened for us.

I noticed that my mother's hands were shaking and I didn't feel too steady myself, so, although our hosts were very pleasant while we got the introductions and formalities under way, I still felt uneasy about the voices in the wind. I even wondered if I should give up the idea of living out there and go back home with my mother in the morning, away from that place of ghosts.

Shortly afterwards the door opened and in came the daughter of the family and her young son. They had been out to Ludag getting some stores from a grocer who came out there in his van. Two other women from Glendale had been with them. We hadn't been aware of them but they had actually followed us all the way. Our detour up the sheep track had worried them, as they could see us in the distance, apparently stomping off into the wilds. They had seen us getting back on course and had tried hard to catch up with us in case we veered off again. Knowing the hill so well, they had no torches, and as we were walking so fast they eventually realised that they couldn't catch up with us and had dropped back; theirs had been the ghostly voices and laughter we had heard. We never told them how they had frightened us into breaking the speed record for hill walking, just smiled and nodded when young Allan said, "I suppose you walk so fast because you come from the city."

I felt a little apprehensive about moving in with a family of strangers, as teenage memories of freezing rooms, starvation and hostile landladies were still fresh in my mind, but I needn't have worried. My lodgings with the MacIntyre family were a sharp contrast to the dreadful humiliating experience I had had during my Fort William days. I was just a child then and two unscrupulous landladies had nearly destroyed my health, my self-esteem and my faith in my fellow human beings. If it hadn't been for the Notre Dame nuns I would have given up on further education completely.

Although my new family lived in a very isolated community, it was obvious from the first meeting that their standards in most things were a good deal higher than those of many a mainland dweller. Their house was comfortably furnished and scrupulously clean and the walled garden at the front was a riot of colour, with flowers of all descriptions. Not for them the common hardy marigold that was a favourite flower in most Hebridean gardens at the time. It could withstand all efforts of the gales to uproot it and indeed was very difficult to shift once it got a hold in your garden. My father hated them. Once he cleared a patch of marigolds, rotovated the bed and planted potatoes in it. The potatoes failed to thrive but he had the best show of marigolds in living memory.

No, the flowers in MacIntyre's garden were of an infinitely more adventurous variety. I remember the name of one: Chincherinchee; it was a little white flower, not particularly striking, but the name stuck in my mind as we had trouble deciding how to pronounce it. There were dahlias, lilies, Michaelmas daisies, foliage plants and flowering shrubs and much more. At the far end of the garden was a large flourishing vegetable plot, and fruit bushes for jam-making were planted against the boundary walls. The wind coming off the bay could be fierce at times, but with a steep hill behind the house and a fairly high rise in front if it, the growing area was well protected.

The MacIntyre family had been a large one but only a widowed daughter, Kate Ann, and her youngest son lived with the parents in my time. The rest of the family were living on the mainland, and by the positions they had attained it was obvious that the isolation of their home had not hampered their natural abilities in any way. The parents, although old and showing the physical signs of having worked hard all their lives, were still active and of lively minds, and I remember evenings spent discussing many interesting subjects and never a hint of idle gossip. Come to think of it, they'd had so many young teachers boarding with them over the years that there must have been many stories to tell, but not a word was ever said about them. Total integrity.

The school was only a five-minute walk away and I could look out of my bedroom window and see it there silhouetted against the bay. In addition to the cream-painted school with its porch, there was a grassy playground, a small storage building, two outside lavatories and a coalhouse. Coal was provided by the County and was shipped out once a year. The one-roomed school had a little stove and in the winter Kate Ann lit a fire there first thing each morning and left a full box of coal so that I could keep it going for the duration of the school day. She also cleaned the school and made up the National Dried Milk, to which every child in the country was entitled as a mid-morning drink, even if cows with fat udders surrounded the school.

Tins of the powdered milk were stored in the stationery cupboard, as were supplies of books, chalk and other necessities. I thought that this was a strange arrangement, as the cupboard wasn't very big, but when I asked Kate Ann if it might not be better to put them in the storage building outside she laughed and said, "Perhaps in ten years' time! Come. Let me show you." When we opened the door I couldn't believe it. The whole shed was stuffed from floor to ceiling with large cardboard boxes each containing twelve dozen toilet rolls. There had been a clerical error some years previously and someone, either a teacher in Glendale or a dispatch clerk in Inverness, had ticked the wrong quantity on a form. The result was that Neil Campbell's boat had to make two trips across the bay to deliver the goods, and by the time I left the school my few little pupils had hardly made any impression on the contents of the shed.

At first it was strange teaching such a small group of children, but as they were all at different levels we certainly found more than enough work to fill the day, and they were a delight to teach. Although they were accustomed to seeing me out of school, once they came in through the door it was strictly business. They were totally formal in their approach to me and to each other in the classroom. If a brother stepped out of line his sister would have no scruples about drawing the matter to my attention: "Michael John MacPhee is not doing his work, Miss." Not "My brother . . ." So they practised the etiquette that they would one day use in their workplace.

Wherever you find a teacher you will find stories about children, some funny and some just plain boring. I have no funny stories about the children in South Glendale School. It was a long time ago and the children were serious and well behaved, most unlike the tough cookies with whom I'd had dealings in Glasgow.

One child called Mary at St John's, Gorbals, comes to mind, a little six-year-old going on fifty. We had just finished a lesson on Good Manners and the class had been instructed to write a few lines on how they could be pleasant to people. Mary came out to me and said: "Gie's a pencil!", to which I replied in a slightly reproving voice: "Go back to your seat, Mary. Think about the lesson we've just had. Then ask me properly."

Mary sat down for a few minutes and then came out to the desk and said in a louder voice: "Ah ken what to say. It's gie's a pencil, MISS."

Flushed with partial success, I patted her hand and said: "Nearly there, Mary. Just take a few more minutes to think about it and ask me again."

Soon she was back tugging my sleeve. "Do you know what to say now?" I asked, confident that at least one of the forty would become a better person through my efforts.

"Yes!" said Mary. "Keep yer bloody pencil!"

We had a long talk at playtime about that incident, but I doubt if Mary saw the point of it all.

Catherine, my teacher aunt, told me her favourite school story from the days when she was a pupil teacher at Garrynamonie School with Fred Rea, author of *A School in South Uist*. She was teaching a little girl her alphabet, using the old way, which has just been rediscovered by the education establishment. We called it "Chalk and talk"; they call it "Teaching phonics by rote". She wrote the alphabet up on the blackboard and, pointing to the letter "o", she asked one little girl to identify it. She was given the right answer but then she tried "a" and the little girl said, "*Cearc*" (a hen). I suppose the letter does look like a little fat hen.

"No," said auntie, "it is an 'a'."

Next day she tried again and the little girl said: "*Bha thu fhèin ag ràdha 'gur e 'a' a th' ann, ach tha mise cinnteach gur e a th' ann ach cearc*" ("You were saying that it is an 'a', but I'm still sure that it's a hen").

Strange the things you remember.

Over the years I have heard snippets of information about some of my ex-pupils and they have become a cross-section of society, with some rising to great heights and some others doing the best they can. Sadly, last year a young Bristol man whom I had taught briefly towards the end of my teaching days was convicted of a dreadful murder and put away for life. It doesn't do to imagine that as a teacher you are making a lasting impression on young lives. A child like Mary or a few turns on playground duty soon cures that illusion.

During my first year in Glendale we had some exciting news. At last, after years of waiting, the children of the Western Isles were to be allowed to learn how to read and write their own language in the primary schools instead of having to wait until they

24

went to secondary school. There was one snag, however: the teachers already in service, myself included, had not been trained to teach it at primary level. At my own college we had had an old man called Nicky, who came in for one hour every week and rambled on at us about ancient Gaelic bards and stuff like that, but I'm afraid he lost me roughly five minutes after I first met him and I wrote all my letters during his session. As I recall, there was nothing in his lectures about the finer points of teaching a five-year-old who probably thinks an "a" is a hen, that in Gaelic "bh" is pronounced like "v" in English or the concept of broad and slender vowels following each other selectively.

A young Adviser was appointed and he toured the schools, monitoring the Gaelic teaching programme and generally asking us which approach we thought would work. A bit like the blind leading the blind, really. He got very excited about the Glendale children. They had made a papier-mâché and raffia croft house with little plasticine animals and people, all labelled appropriately, in Gaelic. Every day the children moved the little characters around, creating story plots around them and using this time to learn the shapes of basic words from their own environment. The young Adviser was very impressed and spent a whole afternoon writing notes and making sketches of the project.

Most classrooms of the period had little in the way of visual aids and the standard decoration was a large map of the world with the British Empire coloured pink and a plastic-coated poster depicting the Life Cycle of the Butterfly, courtesy of Shell Oil. Interactive education was still in its infancy and project work in the primary school was a very new idea, so at the next meeting of the EIS (the Educational Institute of Scotland) I was gratified to hear the Gaelic Adviser talk at length about the virtue of using a model croft as a teaching aid. He said that he'd got the idea from a little school "at the back of beyond" and I thought it a pity that he could not even remember the name of the school. He certainly remembered the way to "the back of beyond", and during the time I taught at Glendale he showed up many times in his brown corduroy suit and wellingtons. Noticing the frequency of his visits my landlady said: "Why don't you ask Mr Corduroy if he would like to move into the shed with the toilet rolls?"

He always wrote screeds in his notebook, so I suppose that in a small way the children of Glendale played a part in the revival of Primary Gaelic. Either that or, as Kate Ann suspected, Mr Corduroy fancied the teacher.

For the first two years after graduation teachers were classed as probationers and had numerous unheralded visits from the Schools' Inspectorate. They would drop in unannounced, sit in a corner of your classroom and watch you teach for a morning or an afternoon. They would then look at the children's exercise books, the teacher's lesson forecast and record of work, attendance register, logbook, stationery ordering records and so on. They must have been trained to intimidate, as I have never met a teacher who enjoyed their visits. The inspectors were always male. They would speak to you as little as possible and give you no indication of their findings. When the inspection was over they would sweep out of the classroom with barely a nod towards the children, who by then would be thoroughly cowed and acting like little zombies. The teacher would be so light-headed with relief at having survived that she wouldn't be able to remember which part of "goodbye" came first. I wished my first Inspector "Bye-good"!

Fortunately for me, I had an angel on my shoulder: Neil Campbell. The inspectors never walked the hill; when they were ready to pounce they booked Neil's boat, usually a few days in advance, and approached the school by sea. Neil would either call MacIntyres' or, if the inspector was coming on a Monday morning and I had gone home for the weekend, he would phone me there and tell me at what time to expect the visitor, finishing the call by saying, "If you are not ready for him, hang something on the school fence. I'll take him twice around the bay and blame it on the tide."

I never had to send the boat on a circular tour, but the kindness behind the warning was well appreciated.

The only thing I found a bit strange when I first joined the MacIntyre household was being treated like a lady. In Gaelic we use the plural of "thu" (you) and say "sibh" (you plural) when addressing someone who by reason of age or status is our superior. At the age of twenty I found it difficult to have Flora and Calum MacIntyre and their daughter Kate Ann Alexander using the plural "sibh" when talking to me. They were all superior to me in age and wisdom. Although I tried to change this mode of address at first, it was a waste of time. This had always been their courteous way of

27

speaking to their teacher lodgers and I just gave up. I insisted on trying to lend a hand around the place in the evenings, as I couldn't imagine just sitting there acting like a lady while they waited on me, but although I was allowed to set the table, washing the dishes was considered to be beneath my dignity.

One evening, Kate Ann was late home, so I volunteered to bring the cows home for milking, and after some argument off I went. The crofts at Glendale were all steep, as they were part of the hill behind the houses, but the cows were docile as I rounded them up and with Captain the dog delivered them to the byre. Calum stood there waiting, not too happy about my being seen doing menial work for him and I could hear him complaining to himself: "*Nach ann an seo a tha 'n gnothach, an tidsear a' toirt dhachaigh nam beathaichean.*" ("This is a strange business, the teacher bringing the cows home").

Then he saw us and slapping his thigh he bellowed with laughter: "*Càit 'eil sibh a' dol le crodh Alasdair?!*" ("Where are you going with Alasdair's cows?!").

I was sure I had the right beasts, but to a horn they all belonged to his neighbour. Things loosened up after that and, from time to time, with a twinkle in his eye, he'd say: "*Cuiribh an tidsear a dh'iarraidh nam beathaichean a-nochd. Tha mi searbh a' bleoghainn an aon fheadhainn.*" ("Send the teacher for the cows tonight. I'm bored with milking the same ones").

The fresh sea air blowing from the bay gave me a great appetite and Kate Ann was a very good cook and baker. If it hadn't been for all the walking and the dances, I'd have been enormous. Most of the produce in the pantry came from Finlay MacDonald's travelling shop and had to be carried over the hill from Ludag. (I never heard the women complain about the heavy weights they carried in sacks on their shoulders every week.) There was also a shop at South Lochboisdale, again accessible by a long walk over rough ground. However, Kate Ann's garden provided fruit, vegetables and potatoes, and there was always a variety of fish and shellfish to supplement the meat from the van and the occasional slaughtered sheep or chicken. When one of the young males in the family came home for a visit, the gun came out and we had game birds to add to the variety. We ate very well. I had my first taste of *sgarbh* (cormorant) and *naosg* (snipe). I don't know if either of these birds was a protected species at the time; all I know is that the villagers of South Glendale had to endure far more than anyone who makes laws and they richly deserved to take whatever nature offered.

It really annoyed me to see causeways being constructed and existing roads being resurfaced to take the weight of Army vehicles, while out in Glendale a short stretch of road running out from Ludag would change so many lives. The villagers told me that many letters and petitions had been sent to the County and nothing had happened. So I passed the winter evenings writing letters to all and sundry, some pleading, some angry and some downright rude, all with the same theme: the road. Sometimes I collected signatures and Flora would say, "*Mura leig sibh fois air na daoine, cliòraidh iad a-null a dh'Eirisgeigh sinn*" ("If you don't stop bothering them, they will clear us over to Eriskay").

She didn't really believe this, but like me she could see that the letters, like the many written before my time, were having no effect.

I wrote a particularly sarcastic letter to the Member of Parliament for the Western Isles, asking him how he would like to live like a tortoise carrying all his household supplies on his back over a hill his entire life, but again it brought no reply. However, a few months after I had finished my time at Glendale School, Kate Ann phoned to tell me that the Member of Parliament had just visited them and wanted to meet Mr MacMillan — I had just signed the letter with my initials and he had automatically assumed that I was male. Although I was only a few miles away at Daliburgh School, he didn't call in to see me, and from what I gathered, the villagers of Glendale had been given the same old story: the road was on the agenda, but a starting date for commencement of work had not yet been finalised.

CHAPTER
THREE

Decorating they call it now. Then we called it "Doing up the room". I had just spent a precious weekend giving our bathroom at home a face-lift: red marbled Fablon halfway up, a border and white paint round the rest of the walls. The builders had painted it pink in something called distemper, and every time you wiped a mark off the wall, the cloth was full of pink gooey stuff. After many years in a little thatched cottage without any kind of bathroom, my mother wasn't fussed about the decoration at first, but five years on it was getting on her nerves. My father did all the preparation, and when I'd finished doing my bit he declared himself so pleased with the results that from then on he was going to ignore the rest of the house and live in the bathroom.

I think that was the moment I realised that I really enjoyed "doing up a room", and since then I have added to the profits of DIY stores in whichever part of the world I happened to be living. Only once have I volunteered to inflict my services on someone else, and to this day I'm not entirely sure how it all came about.

Shortly after the bathroom weekend I happened to be visiting the Steeles, in a house not far from our own, where we were always welcome to drop in and have a cup of tea, a gossip and perhaps a game of cards if we could make up the numbers for "Catch The Ten". Donald James Steele was an elderly man who had married a younger woman, Mary Ann, in middle age. His eldest child, Calum, was only a few months younger than I was, and so I always remember Donald James as an older man. Wives who married older men in that era often found that they had to do both inside and outside work on the croft in addition to bringing up a family and in Mary Ann's case there was an even older, bedridden sister of Donald James's and two Irish packmen lodgers to look after. By the time the children were into their teens, the sister-in-law had died and one of the packmen, Peter Jordan, had moved on, leaving his brother Willie to become quite a dominant part of the family for the rest of his life. Mary Ann coped with it all and never seemed to lose her sense of humour in what could never have been an easy household.

On the night in question Willie was carrying Donald James, who was recovering from a bad stroke, up the stairs to his bedroom. His was the strongest back in the house and he didn't seem to mind helping out — in fact Mary Ann told me that he did this morning and night without even being asked. I must have said something along the lines of "Why don't you let Donald James sleep downstairs in the closet? It would make getting him into the living room so much simpler for you."

"The closet is a Glory Hole," said Mary Ann. "It hasn't been used since his sister Flora died some years ago. The whole place is so dark and horrible that I can hardly see to clean it any more."

At that point I must have said, "Why don't we do it up?"

She took me in there and I could see what she meant. It was dark! There was a reasonably sized window and the room itself was a lot larger than the small room in the thatched croft house commonly known as the closet. Steeles' was a two-storied stone-built house, a sign of past prosperity, but the march of time had well and truly tramped all over the closet. However, I could not withdraw my offer, especially when Mary Ann said, "I'll get the boys to wash the walls down and get some paint and paper in, and we can do it up the next time you're over from Glendale."

So that's how I found myself up a ladder with a paintbrush in my hand and Willie Jordan standing at the foot, offering me a dram and telling me that I was a saint.

Willie, as I have mentioned, was a packman who travelled all over the island selling clothes. During his long tenure of one of the Steeles' rooms he had become accepted as part of their family, godfather to their children, and had assumed at least as much authority in the house as its owners. His legendary tall tales, mostly of Irish valour and the superhuman strength of his father, are still remembered by all who knew him. The mammoth drinking binges he enjoyed, although infrequent, were always memorable and made his name known to all. By now age had taken its toll and more often than not he preferred to drink at home when the urge came upon him. He would go to Polachar Inn, have a tot at the bar and bring a bag of bottles home with him. Then he would close the door of his room and disappear from the world for a week or so. Not as spectacular as his behaviour of previous years, when he and his chosen drinking companions could be on the razzle for days or even weeks non-stop, but a lot safer, as even when he was stone-cold sober his driving was becoming erratic. Nobody begrudged him his peculiar "package holiday", and as he was never noisy, violent or in any way abusive, the Steeles simply turned a blind eye and waited for him to appear at the breakfast table again when it was over.

Somehow the "doing up of the closet" and the thought that his services as hospital orderly would no longer be required prompted the desire for a celebration. He contacted my father, himself not averse to a drop at the time, and invited him to come along for the ride. For many years they had indulged in verbal sparring as Willie told his crazy stories and my father tried to disprove them, yet throughout that time they remained the best of friends. Off they went to Polachar Inn and I got on with the painting.

It was the first time I had ever used a roller and, having painted round the edges and corners with the brush first, I was amazed at the speed with which this new gadget transformed the khaki-coloured surfaces. The brilliant white ceiling lit up the whole room. While the first coat was drying I measured up the rose-sprigged paper that Mary Ann had chosen and together we matched and pasted and hung. She wiped the newly finished sections of wall to get rid of the air bubbles while I, having the stronger head for heights, took care of the lining up and all the rest of it. It didn't take long, and the light bright room that was gradually emerging spurred us on.

Now and then Mary Ann would go out of the room and come back in again just to see the effect; it must have pleased her as she kept saying "Well, well!" in a happy tone.

This is a common Hebridean observation, and can be used to convey all kinds of emotions, depending on which tone of voice is used. Towards evening, with the papering done and only the woodwork to paint and a second coating of the ceiling (which had dried to a slightly patchy finish due to my lack of expertise with the roller) to do, we decided to call it a day. Promising to come back on the next day to finish the job, I went home, had a bath and went to bed.

The next day being Sunday, we all went to church, and only after we got back home did I hear about the spectacular ending to the Polachar run. My father was saying, "Never again!" in the time-honoured manner. I didn't pay much attention at first, but then I heard him telling my mother that Willie had been relatively abstemious at the pub — just a few halves of Bell's and a few half-pints of beer or, as the locals called this, a half and a half. Then he bought the usual dozen bottles of whisky to take out and they left for home. Willie had been driving very well and they had been within sighting distance of Steeles' when he turned the car over. That car had been turned over so often that the roof would have been the more logical place for the bumper. However, the luck of the Irish always hovered round Willie and neither passengers nor driver were ever hurt.

This time he had pulled over right on the edge of a steep grassy bank to allow a tractor coming towards him to pass, got into an argument with my father about the identity of the tractor driver and put his foot on the accelerator instead of the brake. The car shot down the bank and turned over. The door on my father's side had swung open on impact and he practically fell out, but the driver's door had jammed shut and in my father's words: "Willie was squashed between the back of the seat and the top of the car like a big bluebottle" (meat fly).

He pushed and shoved his friend's considerable bulk out of the car and told us that at that stage he really thought that Willie had breathed his last.

"Once the air hit him he started to twitch and moan and then he opened his eyes," said my father. "Then at last he stood up, a bit unsteadily and obviously very put about; he was mouthing something at me but I couldn't understand him, so I asked him to point to where the pain was."

"Bejasus, Norman, don't bother me about pain at a time like this," he answered. "Go and make sure that the bottles are OK!"

Willie had only been winded but, as usual, he knew where his priorities lay.

I left my parents speculating on how many more rollovers the "*cars beag*" (Willie's Irish version of little car) and its driver could survive, and went off to finish my painting job. As it happened, the Austin was scrapped shortly after that and Willie bought a shiny green van. He was so enamoured of it that he drove it to St Peter's Church and got the priest to bless it. On the way out of the driveway, he ran down two of the priest's hens and caused the housekeeper to have a rant at him.

Willie as usual had an answer: "Sure, and I only sacrificed the poor craythurs in thanks for the blessing!"

The van didn't get treated any better than the Austin, but actually outlived Willie.

When I arrived at Steeles' on that Sunday morning, Mary Ann was doing something round the byre, and as Hebridean houses, even now, are seldom locked, I just went straight on in and got on with painting the ceiling. I noticed that the door had been painted earlier on that morning, probably by one of the sons, and I decided that they could also do the window frames, as I didn't like working with gloss paint. The second coat of paint covered the ceiling well and I worked more slowly with the roller this time to ensure a more even finish. I expected a nice quiet morning with the lodger safely tucked up in his own room with his stash and I nearly fell off the ladder when he appeared at the foot, bottle in one hand and glass in the other, and began to extol my virtues.

"*Ciorstaidh nighean Tormod, 's e naomh à Flathanas tha innte. Bidh Donald James cho toilichte às na rooms beag brèagha seo 's gum bih i beò gu bràth!*" ("Christina, Norman's daughter, she is a saint from heaven. Donald James will be so happy in these little pretty rooms that she will live for ever").

Nobody could attempt a correct translation of Willie's pidgin Irish/Scottish Gaelic, but that is a fair attempt. His long association with the island had resulted in his speaking a peculiar dialect of his own, with gender confusion and bits of English thrown in. Once you caught the gist it was fairly easy to follow, and to correct him earned you a glare worthy of the Princess Royal, followed by what can only be described as a long sulk.

When I got over the initial shock of his presence and refused the offer of a whisky to give me strength, I got on with my job and Willie, delighted to have a truly captive audience, started to fill me in on his version of the previous day's adventure. He was very annoyed about a woman who had come to the scene of the accident to see if she could be of any help: according to Willie, she was just being nosy.

"Mrs Morrison, he was very worried. He thought we were dead. When she saw that we were alive, did he try to help us? Not a finger did he lift to try and get the car back on the road. He just kept telling me that it was time I stayed at home and behaved myself. He said that I could have hit a cow or killed a child or even sent Norman and myself to the other side. I told him that when I was driving planes back in the old country I could land one on Barnacle Rock if the tide was out. My driving has never been better. Sure, and if I do go in a ditch now and then, I do it slowly, and if people keep their cows off the road I won't go into the byres and try to kill them."

I had heard most of Willie's stories several times and thought, "This is where he tells me the story of the cattle rustler his father caught and killed by throwing a bull at him," so I tried to head him off by saying, "So you and Mrs Morrison won't be friends any more then."

"No, not at all! That's not the way of it, sure, I made it up with him. I was busy trying to get the car sorted, so I put my arm round her and told her to go home, sit down on a nice soft chair and smoke a pipe."

Mrs Morrison was very much a proper lady and the thought of her smoking even a cigarette made me laugh so much that I nearly fell off the ladder. Unfortunately, Willie took this as encouragement and joined in with his own wheezy laugh punctuated with fits of coughing and embarked on further stories till Mary Ann came in and added her own bits of information about the accident. Willie didn't like sharing a platform and left us to it as he dragged himself off the newly painted door, which now bore the perfect imprint of his back in Harris Tweed fibres. Needless to say, the jacket had not fared any better than the door, and although he sent it to the cleaners later on that month, they could not remove the pink paint and it had to be thrown away in the end.

Mary Ann and Donald James had three children, and my young brother Donald shared many teenage scrapes with their eldest son Calum, who worked in a garage and had an old motorbike. Although his mother was pretty unflappable about most things, she really worried about his safety on the bike, and we talked about this as we cleared up the bits of wallpaper, deciding to leave Calum to repair the damage inflicted by Willie on the door.

A few nights before, the boys had crashed the bike. The lights had failed and they had run into a sheep, which had been wandering about on the main Daliburgh-Kilpheder road, between the crossroads and A. C. MacDonald's shop. I think the poor sheep was killed but both the boys were extremely lucky, as one was thrown into a ditch and the other landed on some packing material outside MacDonald's store; the first boy was extremely wet and smelly and the other had a few scratches, but had they landed on the tarred road they would have shared the same fate as the sheep.

I pretended to know nothing about the incident, as I had only heard my brother's story and I wanted to hear what Calum had told his mother. Mary Ann went on to tell me his version, which although close enough to the truth was still far enough away from it to make me realise that some of Willie Jordan's gift for exaggeration had indeed rubbed off on his godson.

"Calum told me," she said, "that Donald shot off the pillion, over his shoulders, and landed inside a tea chest by A. C. MacDonald's shop, standing on his head. The crash was not their fault at all. They were riding very slowly as the lights were bad, only doing ten miles an hour, and along came this sheep doing sixty . . ."

I'm afraid I was more inclined to believe that Willie Jordan had been an airline pilot in Ireland than that tale of supersonic sheep, but that was before I became a mother myself and learned how gullible you can be when your child spins a tale.

The closet was a great success and Donald James was really pleased to be so near the rest of the family and less trouble to anyone. He was an exceedingly gentle, dignified man, and the thought of putting anyone out was only marginally less hurtful to him than being seen to be in such a helpless state. Even on days when he was not well enough to leave his bed, everyone who came to the house had to pass by his door and he would call out *The latha math!*" ("It's a fine day"), the Hebridean equivalent of "Hello!", so he had a steady stream of visitors and kept up with the comings and goings in what was always a busy house.

In the evenings, especially, Steeles' house was always full of people. Willie, being the Marks and Spencers of Kilpheder, kept his packs in his bedroom and there were always plenty of customers wanting to buy goods which were not available elsewhere. The bench was never empty and Mary Ann greeted each newcomer cheerfully and moved the kettle to the hottest part of the stove ready for the next cup of tea. She had lived her life and brought up her family with a lack of privacy which would have driven most of us mad, but seemed none the worse for it. When business with Willie was over and done with, the evening usually ended with a few hands of cards, and the game was always "Catch The Ten".

I have spent many years telling people that "Catch The Ten" is a game played only in the Hebrides until I looked at a book of card games last year and found it as the subtitle for a game called "Scotch Whist". That should have alerted me, as we all know that all things belonging to Scotland are either Scottish or Scots and that Scotch comes in a bottle. On reading the rules of play, however, I came back to my original conclusion: "Catch The Ten" is a game played only in the Hebrides.

I have no idea where the game originated and I have never seen it played away from the islands, but in the Uists of the 1960s and before, even the oldest card player knew of it and could play it with razor-sharp skill. Think Partner Whist played with a depleted pack and a bucketful of added rules and you've got it. Add a Tilley lamp and a few drams and you are practically winning the game: you play only with cards numbered 6 and above. If there are six or eight players you need two packs. Players play as partners, and if there is an odd number, a dummy hand is dealt. The player who is the dummy's partner plays its hand, but keeps it closed. The general pattern of play is similar to whist, but there are differences both in strategy and scoring.

The Trump face cards all carry points: Ace 4, King 3 and Queen 2. The Jack of Trumps is the strongest card in the pack, carrying a score of 13, unless it is the only Trump card on the table at the end of a round, when it is "Hung" and only scores 1 point. (This is usually accompanied by much jeering and crowing from the opposition.) The Ten carries 10 points but can be overtrumped by any of the face cards. (If it is done by an opponent the jeering and crowing are again brought into play.) If the player on your right slips the Ten in and you are also short-suited, then you can risk trying to "catch" it with a Trump face card. Make it a good one, however, as the player on your left can be in a similar situation to your own and by playing an even stronger face card take your points scorer and keep his partner's Ten safe.

The first pair to reach a score of 42 points wins the game. The number of tricks gained by each pair also counts, and you can score 5, 6 or 10 by cards, but the greatest feat of all, as rare and prestigious as a golfer's "hole in one", is a "Vaul". This happens when one pair gain all the honours and all the tricks. Even if their opponents have had the better score up till then, their scores are wiped out and the couple that have successfully engineered the "Vaul" are undisputed winners. Forgive me if I have got any of the details wrong. It has indeed been a very long time since I "tried this at home", and it is a great but quite complicated game.

I think every member of our family played cards at Steeles' at one time or another. There was never any money involved: we simply enjoyed pitting our wits against the skill and strategic play of the masters. My father claimed to know when Mary Ann had the Jack in her hand; she would tell the dealer off for giving her rubbish and whistle "Hò rò, 's gur tù mo rùn", an old Gaelic melody, under her breath, he said. However, she

43

found out what he'd been saying and, like all good poker players, used the tune to confound the opposition when she really did hold a handful of rubbish.

Cards were played mostly on winter evenings when it was dark early and outside work no longer possible. Now we have streetlights on various roads, but in the old days when the sun went down the darkness was so total that you could feel it. A torch was a necessity if you were going out. If the wind was really howling outside, a ghost story or two would follow the card game at Steeles'. Everybody knew one, and as people drew closer to the stove they tried to put off the moment when walking home in the dark made the stories at which they had scoffed a few minutes previously seem ever more credible.

On such a night my mother was walking home having done some business with Willie Jordan. It was a wild night, and as there had been a funeral that morning, the card game had been suspended, so she stayed for a chat with the family and Willie came down to join them. He kept talking about a light which he had seen hovering over the crossroads between our house and theirs. He said that he had seen it several times hovering above the crossroads, then moving on down over the canal bridge and past the church to the cemetery on the machair. Mary Ann said, "Away with you, Willie, it was probably the priest's housekeeper going home from somewhere that you saw, and then maybe some Daliburgh boys were out on the machair rabbiting."

Talk went on to the funeral and how old people still believed that a spade which was to be used to dig a grave always moved around by itself a few days before the person died. This was common belief in my grandparents' day. If you saw a spade jumping about you, got the black shawl out. There were many other ways of forecasting death — a cockerel crowing in the middle of the night, a dog howling for no reason and the absolutely foolproof one: someone seeing a vision of you wearing a shroud.

Mary Ann had been talking about a woman from Boisdale from days gone by who had been saying farewell to her son before he went off fishing in his boat. She saw his clothes change into a winding sheet before her eyes, and when she tried to touch him her hand felt wet as if water separated them. She begged him not to go out on his boat that day, and after he heard what she had seen he agreed to stay at home. As he couldn't go fishing, he did some jobs around the byre and cleaned the little house used by the chickens and ducks. When it was time for him to come in for his dinner, his mother went to fetch him and found her son lying face down in the duck pond. He'd tripped and fallen in, hitting his head on a rock, and had drowned in six inches of water. Other ghoulish topics were touched upon, and by the time my mother, always a nervous person in the dark, left for home she was well and truly spooked.

The torch was a good strong twin-cell bicycle lamp and my mother walked along using the light to avoid puddles as she braced herself against the strong wind.

The thought of Willie's phantom light made her nervous, and as she approached the crossroads she tried to think of anything in the world except ghosts. When she felt two hands in the small of her back she was so terrified that she couldn't even scream. The torch fell crashing to the ground and she ran faster than she ever thought she could, losing both her shoes and caring nothing for puddles. She ran right past our house and only slowed down when she saw the headlights of a car coming towards her. Drawing courage from the strong beam of light, she turned and looked over her shoulder. There lolloping after her was Collie, our old dog. He had been waiting for her at the crossroads and when she'd hurried past him he'd given her a gentle push with his paws to let her know that he was there to guard her. Judging by the colour of my mother's face when she came in all bedraggled and shoeless, I think a few spades in Kilpheder had been taking tentative little jumps that night.

CHAPTER
FOUR

The Machair where Willie Jordan's phantom torches were last seen was originally bordered by a stretch of high sand dunes along the west side of the island, sheltering the good growing soil behind it and providing a buffer between the crofts and the winds blowing in off the Atlantic. Once the tall craggy outline had been a distinctive feature of the Uist coastline; over the years, however, natural erosion and the needs of island builders have decimated the dunes where we used to play our sliding games and have Sunday picnics in the white hollows.

Each crofter had an acreage of machair land designated as part of his croft and in my childhood years it formed a valuable section of our own crop-growing land. Wheat, barley, oats and potatoes thrived there, needing little maintenance. The parts of the croft closest to the house were used for haymaking, growing more potatoes and vegetables, and a large area was used solely for cattle grazing. The crofters also had some land out in the wetter areas where they dug peat for fuel and the hills were common grazing ground for their flocks of sturdy little black-faced sheep.

The machair croft had a magical quality when we were children. We went down there to help with the harvest and could play in the sand and wade in the sea when the work was done. Later, when Dr Kissling and Tom Lethebridge unearthed the remains of an early civilisation with their local helpers, we joined the many tourists marvelling at this piece of the past which had turned up on our doorstep, so to speak. Sadly, neither the owners of the island nor any other establishment have organised any means of preserving that valuable historical find, and now the fine white sand of the machair is once again giving the second-century wheelhouse a decent burial.

Once tourism took hold, we had the odd hippy-type camper trying to have a "back-to-nature" holiday experience on the machair and giving up the second or third time he had to retrieve his tent from a wildly frothing Atlantic in the middle of the night. Pitching a tent in a hollow was no answer either. The shelter of the dunes would keep the tent from blowing away, but as night storms are generally accompanied by torrential rain, the hollow would soon become a little loch and the camper and his worldly goods would get very soggy. Neither of these weather conditions were enough to deter the British army, however, and shortly after the plans for a Guided Weapons Range in Iochdar had passed muster and a small barracks had been established in Benbecula, we had soldiers swarming all over Kilpheder machair.

The island had already seen a temporary influx of RAF personnel during the Second World War years and many fond memories of the "airmen" remained. They had been based at Balivanich in Benbecula and had played a very important part in the defence of Britain's North Atlantic coast. The Air Ministry had bought the north end of Benbecula in 1942, and the airport and the work it provides have served the islands well over the years.

Despite this favourable history, the islanders were not too impressed when the Ministry of Defence first started making plans for their range. Aided by Father John Morrison, parish priest in Iochdar, himself born and bred in Kilpheder, people were made more aware of their rights and the crofters could see that the testing of guided missiles on the island could have many negative aspects. The main objection was that machair crofting land would be lost in Gerinish and Iochdar where the range and its maintenance buildings would be situated. Benbecula people did not want Balivanich to become militarised and the local business community were anxious in case their livelihoods would be under threat if the army built their customary large NAAFI shops and opened the doors to the general public.

Over a period of time, agreements were, however, reached, people were compensated and assurances were given that the range and camp were not going to be used as a military training base as such. A small friendly presence of personnel, testing the "rockets", didn't pose any threat and so the Army moved in. Well, over the years Balivanich did become militarised and the sprawling monolith of the army barracks changed the township's character and appearance dramatically, and, certainly during the Falklands conflict, troops were trained there.

Still, there were many positive aspects to the second coming of the men in uniform: better roads, more jobs, more children for the schools, the first cinema and a real chemist's shop in Balivanich, to mention but a few. As far as my father and his peers were concerned, the most positive effect the soldiers on Kilpheder machair had on their lives was that their bar tent was open to all and sundry, with drinks at NAAFI prices, seven days a week.

I was living in Glendale from Monday till Friday and was far too concerned with doing my job and coping with inspectors, while taking an active part in the social activities of my islander peer group, to have much indepth knowledge of what the soldiers were actually doing. From the road I could see many large green marquee-type tents of the kind that shall be moved neither by gale nor rainstorm. Camouflaged jeeps and other wagons were a common sight thundering past our house and my mother complained that the dog was in perpetual danger of being flattened. My father remarked that the time to worry would be when tanks with guns and Communist flags started rolling by.

"These are our boys, God bless them!"

He didn't mention the beer but I'm sure it fuelled his patriotic fervour. Our neighbour, John, reported that "They are always having a kind of Highland Games and cooking curry."

50

I still don't know what they were doing on the machair, but assume that it was part of some protracted survival exercise.

I doubt if anybody actually asked the soldiers what the purpose of their presence was. We islanders had become so used to people of all kinds coming to the island and doing exactly as they wanted without consulting us. Our ancestors had been looked upon purely as a financial investment, firstly for the clan chief and then — when he had bankrupted himself through his passion for gambling and a certain Mrs Hall (no relation!) — the subsequent owners followed the same pattern. The original islanders were there to cut and process kelp, which their masters sold for huge sums of money. The workforce had to be kept alive, so each family was given a small piece of land, enough to sustain one cow and one calf. The bottom fell out of the kelp industry and the people were "cleared" to make room for the masters' new investment, sheep. It was not until the end of the First World War that the people of the Uists eventually won the right to rent a proper croft-sized piece of the country for which they had fought so bravely. With that kind of history, it took a long time for us islanders to start asking questions of strangers, in or out of uniforms.

The soldiers didn't bother the people of Kilpheder; they were very friendly and courteous. I am sure they must have been amused by the groups of children who rushed down to the machair after school every day to "look at the Army". One little local lad in particular used to entertain them by singing songs for bottles of

Coca-Cola. He had a voice like an angel and knew every popular English and Gaelic song going, so the show would last as long as the Cokes kept coming. By now the local shops had improved vastly but still tended towards the basics, and although the shop owners could be very generous to people in real need, I doubt if the little lad would have got anything out of them by offering to sing for it.

Before long the bar tent was as popular as any of the local pubs, and on a Sunday when the other bars were closed, men from the north end of the island would be taken by a sudden urge to travel south and make the "boys" feel welcome. I would have liked to have been a fly on the tent wall, as I am sure that the soldiers were told many "facts" of island life that could not always bear scrutiny. Winding up incomers, especially the more gullible ones, has long been a common ploy among some of the younger island men and I'm sure the soldiers came in for their share.

Let me give you a fairly recent example, which took place in the bar of Lochboisdale Hotel, haunt of anglers and gillies during the fishing season. A visiting angler had just finished his dinner and was having a brandy at the bar, when he spotted his gillie drinking with his friends at a nearby table. The gillie is a very valuable asset to any keen fisherman, as he knows where the trout can be found and can row the angler to the best spot. Theirs is a relationship involving mutual respect and often genuine friendship, but not in this case. It was more of a master-servant scenario and the gillie quite rightly resented this. It was the last night of the angler's holiday, so when he came over to their table, second brandy in his hand, to enthuse about the excellence of the prawns he had just eaten, the gillie saw a chance to get his own back. "Yes," he said. "Our prawns are the best in the world. It's because of the corn, but you probably know that."

"The corn?" queried the angler.

"Yes, indeed. The prawns they serve here come from the sea down by the machair. At night when the moon comes up they crawl along the shore and wander on to the machair to eat the corn. There's nothing in the world as tasty as a corn-fed prawn."

"Well, I'll be blowed!" said the angler. "I never knew that."

"Ach, it's got to be a real problem for the poor crofters," said the gillie. "But things are looking up. The EEC has just approved a grant for Prawn Fences to be put up all along the machair."

The angler wandered off to pass on this nugget of information and the gillie and his friends tried to keep a straight face until he was safely out of sight.

The soldiers survived their first taste of Uist and the locals survived the beer. Soon the temporary accommodation was dismantled and the site left, with the efficiency of the Army, as they had found it. The green wagons headed northwards to Benbecula to establish a more permanent base for their rapidly swelling numbers.

Many of the islanders found work with the contractors building the camp in Benbecula, and also in Gerinish and Iochdar, where the firing range was beginning to take shape. Work was also going on in St Kilda, a remote archipelago far out in the west, separated from the Outer Isles by 50 miles of rough sea and populated mainly by rare sheep and seabirds. There the army required a road, a camp and two missile-tracking stations, and my young brother Donald joined some other local men on St Kilda working for the contractors. It was a bit similar to the South Georgia whaling situation, as they lived in a very isolated place for the duration of their contract and came home with a nice lot of money.

Our family had already started to scatter itself far from the croft, and although they all kept in touch, it was a much quieter household than it had been in the days of my childhood. The two older boys, Donald Angus and Donald John, were both in England, now young men establishing themselves in the outside world. Donald Angus's hopes of a Naval career had ended at the age of sixteen, when an accident aboard his first ship resulted in the loss of his left hand. After the rehabilitation period, when the inevitable realisation of all he had lost hit him, he went through a dark time. He was awarded a pitiful sum of money as compensation and used it to blot out the images of what might have been by spending much time in Monte Carlo. On his return he had the good fortune to meet a man who was recruiting trainee management staff for the Railway Hotel syndicate, and although his disability meant that he could never achieve full manager status within that organisation, the training he received put his feet on the right path and gave him a new belief in himself.

Donald John had finished his National Service and joined the Metropolitan Police. He was engaged to an English girl, Brenda Cranstone, from Eweshott. My father had just finished making scathing comments about Scots "marrying out" when Donald Angus phoned to say that he had been seeing a great girl, Sheila Collins, for some time and they were soon to be married.

"From the north, I hope," said my father.

"Yes," said Donald Angus. "Manchester."

Once my father met them they all got along just fine, but he always managed at least one rendition of "Flower of Scotland" during their visits. The twins had also left home: Alick was a horticultural apprentice in a nursery in Carmunnock outside Glasgow, while Mary Flora worked and lived at Daliburgh Hospital for a while and then moved down south to work in Devon.

The custom of naming your children after relatives meant that my mother had three Donalds to commemorate, and she did this by naming her first three sons Donald Angus, Donald John and Donald. The situation was fairly common on an island where many of the people were descendants of the Clan Donald, and as the second names were always used, there was never any confusion.

Young Donald had always been the most helpful member of our family around the croft, and sometimes I feel that much of the work he shouldered, starting as a schoolboy, went unnoticed by my parents, as they always seemed to make much of the ones who had left. Donald was content to take whatever work he could get and fill his spare time with croft work and his music. I was glad of his company when he came home for a while after finishing a job, and when, after a few years, he left home to join the London Fire Brigade, I think my parents finally realised just how much of a support he had been to them.

The accordion was Donald's favourite instrument, although he could pick up any instrument and play it and even make his own. He and two other friends formed a band and called themselves "The Pioneers". Donald found a tea chest and painted a logo on the front — a flaming torch, I think it was — with the name of the band painted around it. One night they were practising in our front room and I could hear a new sound, which blended in very well although it wasn't instantly recognisable: Donald had attached a broomstick and a piece of string to the tea chest and was playing it as a double bass.

The other lads from that practice of long ago are still playing music in Uist, and have established themselves as *Na Deasaich* (The Southerners), a band of some repute. Donald went on to compose the music for "*Tioram air Tir*", his brother Donald John's best-known song, and other melodies. Although still living and working in London, he likes nothing better than to play the lovely Highland tunes with a couple of bands in his spare time. He still plays a diverse number of instruments, the latest being the banjo, although the accordion is still his first love.

While I was at Glendale my father was still as busy as ever with concerts and recording, and one occasion he bullied me into my own first public performance as an adult. He finished his last song and announced that I would sing the next one. I was sitting in the audience at St Peter's Hall and will never forget the way my knees trembled all the way up to the stage. I think anger made my voice strong and I actually enjoyed the applause at the end; I was hooked. After that I performed many times but I never got over the stage fright. However, the backstage camaraderie, and the applause and the buzz of being one of the performers, were fantastic. My father and I often appeared at the same concerts up and down the islands, and often Donald and his friends would also be on the programme or playing for the dance that followed.

My mother, the best singer and musician of us all, sat in the audience. Although she had been a very popular singer in her youth and had won a medal and was also a natural pianist, she suffered from stage fright and quite early on in her married life refused to put herself through the ordeal of being on stage ever again. A pity, really, because I recently came across a song of hers which had been recorded as a filler on one of my father's School of Scottish Studies tapes and the clear sweetness of her voice was pitch-perfect.

I think I realised what a consummate performer my father was when I started to share the circuit with him. He could sing anything, from the oldest, heaviest song to the light little satirical topical ditties that he composed himself, almost on the spot, and his memory

57

was amazing. Although he scorned the use of notes or prompts, he never forgot a word or a sequence of verses and could honestly not understand the meaning of stage fright or any kind of nervous reaction to an audience.

One Friday evening I had come home from school and he was outside fixing a stall in the byre. We were both going to Balivanich Hall that night to take part in a concert. Calum Kennedy was touring the islands and was top of the bill. To this day I would walk over hot coals for a chance to see a young Calum Kennedy performing, so I was practically tongue-tied with terror at the thought of singing on the same stage. I went out to see if my father could give me any tips on conquering my nerves. I'd had my two songs ready for weeks and had been singing them lustily and experimenting with different keys as I walked across the hill to school, to the astonishment of the Glendale sheep. When I approached him, my father was genuinely astonished at my timid attitude.

"What's to be afraid of?" he said. "Just fix your eye on someone in the audience, give them a big smile, open your mouth and get on with it." (It worked.)

I did not disgrace myself that evening and Calum's performance, as usual, was a perfect mix of a great-looking young man, born to wear Highland dress, singing beautiful songs with a voice like velvet soaked in honey. My father, who came on immediately after Calum, got as much applause as the Mod medallist. The audience started laughing and enjoying the prospect of hearing his introductory patter and jokes even before he appeared on the stage. He always gave the audience what he called a "good stirring up" before singing a song, and they loved it. I had asked him what he was going to do, earlier, and had been told, "Good God! I don't know. It's not until this evening and I still have work to do here."

I realised then that, with the exception of a few established stories and songs which he used from time to time, he made it all up as he went along.

That evening he walked on to the stage to resounding applause and waved to someone in the audience. The effect was immediate. Applause faded into silence as they waited to hear what he had to say. He fixed his eye on a woman called Morag and said (in Gaelic) something along the lines of: "It's good to see you here tonight, Morag. I've been meaning to call on you and give you a message from Angus" (the woman's sailor son).

Morag giggled and blushed, knowing that there had been no message but more than willing to be part of the act. After a few moments, when everyone had had a chance to see who Morag was and twitter a little, he carried on: "You thought he was going to South Georgia — well, there was a change of plan. He's just finished a trip way up to the far North." (Another short pause.) "Didn't tell me where, but he's bringing you a penguin, so you'd better put another box in the henhouse and tell the cockerel that he's in for a surprise." (This would get a minor laugh, as the audience knew that there was more to come.)

"Oh, there was another thing: the jersey you knitted for him was lovely. But don't use the hairy Highland wool again. It gives him a terrible itch." Another pause while the audience let their imagination lead them into laughter again.

"He had to throw it away in the end and a polar bear picked it up. I asked him what the bear had done with the jersey. He said that he didn't know where it ended up. The last time he saw it the bear was wearing it and scratching his back against the North Pole."

As the audience, Morag included, laughed away, I could see him looking around for the next target.

Hardly anyone on the island had a television at that time and so I suppose that he was their first experience of audience participation, and they liked it. He'd probably go on to someone else or tell a story with amusing allusions to something that he had just done that day. A bit like Ben Elton's skit about emptying a swing bin, my father found humour in ordinary Hebridean happenings, and as he delivered his version, in his own style, it left the audience speechless with laughter. He was a great singer of traditional songs but he will always be remembered best for his way of "giving the audience a good stir".

On another occasion I was singing at a concert in Iochdar Hall and had finished my encore. The song was "O Mhàiri", a rather slow mournful song that I loved, better suited to a first number. When I was more experienced I realised that the audience prefer a short, fast, light song with a swinging chorus for an encore. There were many young people in the hall, so I dumped a few verses in case they got bored. The next person on the programme was a young lady called Rena MacLean. She was late arriving and had just walked into the back room, where we waited for our turn to go on stage, as the MC was announcing her name. She'd had no time to find out what had gone before, and so she went straight up on to the stage and launched into "O Mhàiri", singing every verse. Rena had a voice of great beauty and in other circumstances it would have been a pleasure to listen to her rendition of the song, but the audience, having just heard it once already, could hardly bring themselves to clap at the end and she came off the stage looking very hurt. I told her what had happened and we were both very embarrassed and dreading the thought of returning to the stage to sing "Soraidh Leibh is Oidhche Mhath Leibh" ("Goodnight and farewell") with the other artistes at the end of the concert.

Next on was my father. He walked to the centre of the stage and said, "With the help of my assistants I am very pleased to bring you something new tonight."

The audience sat back and waited, thinking that some conjuring trick was coming, as he had done that once or twice. He composed his features into a solemn mask and started, "O Mhàiri . . .", singing the first verse, while the whole hall, artistes included, erupted with laughter. Then he stopped and signalled for Rena and me to join him on the stage and we sang the last verse of the song together with a great flourish while the audience joined in. When we left him to go on with his usual "stirring up" we heard him say, "Now the next time I'm here, I am going to test you on that song."

I don't think the audience were ever sure whether it had been deliberately staged or not, but it certainly made us feel better about the whole thing.

One of the most memorable concerts in which I was involved was organised by a young lad called Roderick Morrison, and it took place in Castlebay Hall on the Isle of Barra. He gathered a troupe of us together and under the name of "South Uist Concert Party" arranged the venue and transportation across to Barra in Neil Campbell's boat. There were singers, myself included, Highland dancers and a piper. The accordionists were there, my father came along and I had written a short play for the occasion and some of the performers were doubling as actors. It was taking place on a Friday evening and I was to meet the rest of the gang at Ludag jetty after Glendale School had closed for the weekend.

Roderick looked after all the technical details and had everything planned to perfection, but the one thing he could not control was the weather. On Friday morning we woke up to a blanket of snow. The salty air soon turned that to slush, and looking out of the school windows into driving sleet, I could hardly see across Glendale Bay. Things did not look good for the Barra concert and I was very disappointed.

By the afternoon the cloud had lifted a little but the wind was still strong and the sleet showers persisted. Calum and Flora MacIntyre were full of concern and tried their best to make me stay out in Glendale for the night, refusing to believe that even Neil Campbell would attempt to cross the Sound in that weather. It is the only time I remember them talking to me without the usual deference to "the teacher". They were more like parents advising a none-too-bright child.

"You'll be drenched before you're halfway across the hill." "You'll get to Ludag and you'll be the only one there." "You'll have missed the school bus and then you'll be walking home, in this weather, in the dark."

Kate Ann listened with a twinkle in her eye but didn't join in until they had finished, and then she said the thing that nearly swung the balance.

"They say that drowning is a terrible way to die."

Well, all the advice fell on my deaf ears and I struggled against the wind and battled through the slushy heather carrying my bag of stage clothes behind my back to keep the sleet out of it. I slipped and slithered my way across the hill, and as I arrived at Ludag I saw that I was not the only lunatic abroad on that dismal evening. In a parked van singing "Show me the way to go home" was the entire complement of the South Uist Concert Party, and leaning against a shed in his oilskins and waders, grinning from ear to ear, stood Neil Campbell.

"Ach, it's only a shower. It's a warm summer's day in Barra," he said.

I don't know how he did it, but he chugged his boat through the wind and sleet and landed us in Barra and I never once felt a twinge of fear.

The weather in Barra was indeed better, and by the time we had dried off and eaten a big meal prepared for us by the Castlebay School canteen staff we were all ready for action. It was a memorable evening, enjoyed by everyone, and the dance which followed went on well into the night. Even my father, veteran of many a concert, said that he had seldom enjoyed an evening as much, as he danced the canteen ladies off their feet. We passed the few hours until dawn in the hall, talking and dozing on hard chairs, until the good ladies came back to give us some breakfast and wave us off on our way back to Neil's boat. In true Hebridean style, Saturday morning was bright and calm and the sail back uneventful, as we told Neil about the great time we'd had.

The people of Castlebay had packed the hall until it could hold no more, and some had to sit outside on top of a wall to watch the concert through the windows; many had stayed on in the hall after the dance to keep us company and had waved us off clapping and cheering. It's the closest I ever came to knowing what being one of the Beatles must have felt like. All in all, we were all very glad that we had risked life and limb getting there.

With all this going on, I am not surprised that I did not know much about the Army's business on Kilpheder machair. In fact I didn't really notice the Army much at all during the first few years of its existence in Benbecula.

CHAPTER
FIVE

I suppose the most prestigious person ever to drive past our house in Kilpheder must have been the Queen. It was before my return to Uist as a teacher but during the time when I was home from college on holiday, so I'm glad that I was there to witness such an occasion. There was much talk and excitement in advance of the visit and rumours abounded about the possibility of herself and Prince Philip dropping in to have tea in a crofthouse; I think that one was started by housewives who wanted some new furniture, as nothing came of it. The new school at Daliburgh had a nice big hall and this was chosen as the venue for a royal ball.

I would love to be able to say that some of the Royals attended the ball, but I think they preferred to party on the Royal Yacht, as none of them turned up to grace the glittering event. Still, it was a huge success, and I have never seen so many evening dresses and kilts worn to an island dance before or after. The hall was decorated with streamers of red, white and blue and festooned with lights and balloons of the same patriotic colours. We all sang "God Save the Queen" lustily at the beginning and the end. It's a pity they missed it, really.

We were glad that they had chosen to drive through Kilpheder on the way up to the Alginate Industries factory and the Wheelhouses, as it meant that for the first time ever, the Council managed to find the funds necessary to give us a properly tarred road. Previously the road had just been gravelled and in the winter it got very rutted and messy. In the summer cars would send up a cloud of dust, and I doubt if the Queen would have liked that. So the roadmen had to work hard, and when the great day came we were able to stand by the roadside outside our house and stare through the car windows as they glided slowly by. I remember my mother hissing at us "Wave, wave!"

It seemed a bit silly to wave at someone who was just a few inches away from you, but we did it anyway and they waved back, and we stared at them and they stared back. Then we watched as the car glided on over the shiny empty road towards the next group of people standing by their gate in the distance. My mother said "I've just waved to the Queen, outside our house, in Kilpheder."

Her voice was filled with awe, but I had just felt awkward and a little bit embarrassed by it all. I thought that the Queen's complexion was the most perfect I had ever seen and that she was very small and detached-looking. Prince Philip was gorgeous and he looked at us, as we stood there awkwardly, with an expression of curiosity and faint amusement on his patrician face.

My father had a much closer look, as he was presented to the royal couple and had a few words with them. We heard about little else for days, and to hear him speak about the Queen you'd think that she was someone much to be pitied for having such a boring job. Perhaps he was right, and when he impressed upon us the fact that we had been present at the making of history, he wasn't just referring to the fact that the roadmen had actually finished their work on time.

I considered real history to be something that had happened long ago and it had always interested me. I have seldom found a historic time more fascinating than when tales are recounted by people who have actually lived through it. During my time in Glendale I had the pleasure of listening to many old people talking about days gone by. Calum and Flora MacIntyre were fascinating raconteurs, as were their neighbours who came in to visit them and pass the long winter evenings talking. Having spent my childhood being passed from pillar to post between Uist, Benbecula and Barra, my knowledge of what had gone on before my time was sketchy to say the least, and I loved to hear stories of the old days.

The Clearances and the Emigrants were often spoken of, and there were always little interesting bits of information about the tough lives that some relative had faced when landing on the inhospitable coast of a strange country. I began to think about taking up a teaching post in Canada, and trying to track down some descendants of the original emigrants in Cape Breton and Nova Scotia, to see if they could add to the picture, but all plans like that had to be put on hold at least until my probationary period was over. In those days you could not apply for any permanent teaching position if you had not successfully completed your two years of evaluated work. Years later, when I applied for a job in England, despite being qualified, evaluated and much experienced, I had to do another year on probation. Nowadays burglars serve less.

Some of the Glendale families had originally come from Eriskay. Its being a very small island meant that available crofting land was limited and so, when they had married, they moved over to Glendale and set up their own crofts. Naturally they often spoke of the island, reminiscing about the old days and the Eriskay of their parents' era. The legendary Father Allan McDonald's name always cropped up, and although I knew a bit about him, it was from Calum MacIntyre and his neighbours that I learned the most.

Father Allan had come to Daliburgh in 1884 to look after a large and scattered parish, which at that time included Eriskay. Altogether he was responsible for the moral welfare of roughly 2500 people. After ten years of tireless work, trying to improve conditions for his parishioners and their children, his health broke down and the bishop sent him to Eriskay, where the slower pace of life might be more suited to his ailing health. There he continued to be "all things to all men". Apart from conducting religious services in the small ramshackle thatched church of the time, he helped to ensure that proper educational provision was made for the children, visited the sick and needy and was ever mindful of the hazardous occupation of the fishermen.

He battled non-stop to have the church replaced by a stout stone building with a strong slate roof which could withstand the winter storms. The church of St Michael built on top of Cnoc nan Sgrath was opened in 1903 and the fishermen returning home used it as a landmark. Father Allan was always looking to find ways to bring spiritual comfort to the fishermen and on the Feast of Our Lady, in May, he'd have them assemble all the fishing fleet in the harbour and say Mass on board one of the boats.

Sadly, his health did not improve, and two years after the completion of the new church, he died. The anecdote that most moved me was the story about Father Allan's funeral. When the coffin had been laid in the grave, the people of Eriskay told the men who were preparing to finish the job to put their spades down. Father Allan's parishioners moved forward as one and with their cupped hands filled the grave with earth, gently patting the last squares of grass over the top. Such was the love this young man, who died at the age of forty-two, inspired in his people.

Father Allan's life has been well documented, and amongst his many legacies is his own large collection of songs, stories and folklore. The present-day church of St Michael, with its bell rescued from the German battleship *Derflinger* and its altar resting on the bow of a lifeboat from the aircraft carrier *Hermes*, still stands on Cnoc nan Sgrath.

Stories about "Weaver's Castle" or *Stac a' Bhreabadair*, an island off the coast of Eriskay in the Sound of Barra, little more than a rock with the remains of a ruined fort or castle on its summit, were also told, but as there are already many variations of the legend already in circulation, I will leave it at that. It is said to have been a place of banishment and I could imagine no prison more formidable than the tiny rocky island surrounded by crashing waves. Calum and his neighbour used to tease me by making up stories about its history, but always gave themselves away by including a teacher in the grisly ending. Obviously they had perfected this system over the years, with my predecessors.

In addition to historical folklore, they used to talk about strange creatures that could never have existed such as an *each-uisge* (water-horse). The name is similar to sea-horse, but the mythical creature that they spoke of bore no resemblance to the pretty little fairytale sea-horses you find in any good aquarium. The *each-uisge* was half-man, half-horse; he lived in deep lochs and spent his time trying to lure unsuspecting maidens to join him in their murky depths, never to be seen again. He was definitely thought to be a close relative of Satan, and if you should see one in an aquarium, call Security. The old folk told me, with perfectly straight faces, that one lived in a loch between Glendale and South Lochboisdale, on the Hartabhagh side. The last time he had surfaced was long, long ago; I couldn't pin them down on a century, but got the impression that they had all been told the story by their parents.

A young man was herding sheep near the loch, so the story goes, and his sister had gone out to the remote moorland spot to bring him some food. When she approached the loch she saw a young man whom she took to be her brother wading waist-deep in the loch, near the edge of the water. The part of his body she could see was unclothed, and to avoid any impropriety, should he be naked, she called out that she would leave the bundle of food at the water's edge. He did not reply and kept his back to her until she was standing at the very edge of the loch. She called again, and when the man turned around slowly, she could see that it was not her brother but another young man. He had a face like a god and as soon as she met his eyes she was under his spell. She spent some time just gazing into his eyes and then leaned forward to stroke his hair. As she did so she noticed that his thick black hair gradually changed into reeds at the roots. At that moment she heard her brother calling out, "*Each-uisge, Each-uisge!*" ("Water-horse, Water-horse!") The spell was broken and the girl ran back to safety. The Water-horse turned his back on them and sank slowly beneath the water, never to be seen again.

Of course, I didn't believe that story any more than you do, but it still gave me the shivers to think of the reeds. As far as I can make out, the loch they were talking about is one now used as a part of a salmon farm, so if he's still down there the *each-uisge* is well fed.

One night the postman, a man from South Lochboisdale, was over at MacIntyres' and I asked him if he believed in the stories about the *each-uisge*. He said that his mother had told him about it and she never lied to him, so he sort of believed in it. Then he went on to tell me about a man from Daliburgh (again from long, long ago) who was taking his corn to the mill to be ground. The mill was in Milton near the middle of the island. On the way there the man led the horses, as there wasn't enough room for him in the cart with all the corn. When they got to a bend in the road, the horses stopped dead and no amount of coaxing would make them move. They were whinnying and rolling their eyes and he could see they were very distressed. The crofter himself could see nothing unusual. There was a large rock at the side of the road and the man thought that the dark shadow it cast was the cause of alarm, so he took his coat off and put it over the horses' heads, covering their eyes. The horses immediately calmed down and he was then able to go on his way.

When he arrived at Milton he related the story to the miller, who told him that it could have been some supernatural sighting which made the horses nervous. He said that horses have a much more highly developed sense of sight than humans and that it was quite possible that they could see something from another world. The crofter was sceptical and laughed at such nonsense. The miller told him that if it happened again, he should look over the head of one horse, focus out between the ears and he too would see whatever it was. The crofter still refused to believe him. It was gathering dusk and he didn't want to be on the road too late. The cart was now half-empty, as the miller had taken some of the corn as payment, so he climbed into it and urged the horses homewards.

Sure enough, when they came to the bend in the road where the horses had acted strangely, the same thing happened again. By now it was fully dark, and although there were no shadows visible, the horses stopped and began to buck and whinny. The crofter took his coat off and leaned forwards so that he could reach the horses' heads and cover their eyes again. In so doing he just happened to look between the ears of the nearest horse, and there blocking their path was the Devil. With great presence of mind the crofter started to shout out prayers, and in a flash of light the Devil shot into the rock with such force that a crack appeared in the middle, and he disappeared.

Donald, the postman, couldn't tell me what the Devil looked like, but he did tell me where the rock was situated and I checked it out. There was a large crack just where he had told me it would be — not starting or ending at any specific edge as cracks normally do, but just there, as if a knife had been stuck in and pulled downwards and then taken out. I'm certainly not implying that I believed this or any other stories about demonic sightings in South Uist, but remember this rock, as I shall be coming back to it.

Apart from telling ghost stories the, postman had another very important function in my life: he brought me the letters which helped me to keep in touch with my good friends from college days. I had two special friends, Mary and Pat, who had been students in my year group at Notre Dame, and as they were also starting out in their careers, albeit in city schools, it was very interesting to share experiences with them. I must admit that most of our letters were about more frivolous matters, but we also wrote about our jobs and passed on a few tips about teaching.

I really looked forward to hearing from them, as they sent me news of other "Old Girls" and kept up a link with the immediate past. In Glendale the hustle of the city seemed very far away, and although I can't say that I ever missed it all that much, it was nice to keep up with the happenings there. I learnt that our old college was closing down; it had been given university status and was being moved, lock, stock and barrel, out to Bearsden. That made me sad, as I had some good memories of my time there, and often as I walked alone backwards and forwards over the hill, my mind would drift back to student days.

Although the convent atmosphere was nowhere near as all-prevailing as it had been in with the Sisters of Notre Dame in Fort William, the regime was still fairly strict as far as coming in at night went. After all, nuns will be nuns. We had to be in at 7.30p.m. on weekdays and 9p.m. at weekends. Residency was compulsory unless you were a final year student or were over twenty-one. You could get an overnight pass if some relative phoned in and vouched that you were staying at their house for the night, and as the nuns were pretty gullible, that wasn't too difficult to arrange. Suffice it to say that it wasn't as restrictive as it sounds.

The faculty consisted of nuns who were highly qualified in the teaching profession and some lay lecturers, all women. It was constantly impressed upon us that we were going to be in charge of fresh young minds entrusted to us by their parents and we should never forget that responsibility. If we didn't feel up to it, we were told we should leave and try something else. Standards expected in both written and practical subjects were very high, and if you failed in one subject, then failed the resit, out you went. One student in my group failed Psychology in this way towards the end of her final year and got no mercy — she was out. It was a lot more difficult to get into that place than it was to leave it.

Criticism lessons were my own pet hate. During the period that you spent doing teaching practice in a school, a nun would come out and listen to you teaching and then evaluate your lesson. If your performance was deemed to be in any way below par, this could also be a one-way ticket to a job in Woolworth's. Most of the remarks were pretty constructive and I found them helpful, but I was always terrified of losing the nun on the way to school. I have a hopeless sense of direction and usually this didn't matter, as we were assigned to schools in little groups and I just followed the pack on and off buses. However, on the day of your Criticism lesson you left later than the rest of your group and escorted your nun to the school. They didn't get out much in those days and relied solely on their student for a safe journey.

One day I was taking an elderly nun out to a school on the edge of the town and I actually knew where to get the bus, where to get off and which street to walk down to find the school. On the journey the nuns usually spoke about various things and tried to put their student at ease, but I knew that Sister Mary Vianney would be interestingly different. She originally came from some wealthy trade family, chocolates or biscuits, I think, and had been a brilliant English lecturer at the college for many years. Her lectures were never boring and she always spoke like an actor, using quotations as we would use slang, in a booming voice that could be heard all over the building. At the end of a session, instead of dismissing us in everyday words, she would intone something like: "Now fold up your tents like the Arabs and steal away into the night."

When we set off she told me that as she had been to this school before, she would need no directions, and she set off at a brisk trot down to Byres Road where we were to catch the bus. I was trying to keep up with her, carrying my briefcase and hers, wondering how such a large nun could move so fast and trying to hear what she was saying as she kept up a flow of "Old English", waving her big, black umbrella about to emphasise her point.

I nearly fell over her when she suddenly stopped and stuck her umbrella out in front of an approaching bus. I tried to tell her that our bus stop was on the other side of the road, but she ignored me and marched on to the bus. Although I tried again to tell her that we were heading in the wrong direction, she carried on talking about the way Glasgow was changing. The conductor was upstairs collecting fares and I prayed that he would hurry up and get to us so that I could ask him where to get the right bus, as by then we were approaching the city centre. Suddenly, this fact also dawned on the nun.

"We are not on hallowed ground, little one," she informed me, "there's something rotten in the state of Denmark!"

Picking up her umbrella, she marched up to the front of the bus. It was in the days when the bus driver sat in a little glass enclosure and didn't have anything to do with the passengers, as the conductor collected fares, but this was no obstacle to Sister Mary. She banged on the glass with her umbrella until the driver was forced to stop and slide his little window open.

"Coachman, thou art going the wrong way!" she boomed at him.

He looked at her for a minute and replied, "Nah, hen, you're on the wrang bus!"

I think it's the only time I ever saw her stuck for words, and she didn't speak again until we had arrived at the school, on the right bus.

College holidays were longer than the school holidays we had been used to, and most of us took advantage of the long summer break to earn some money in any job we could find. I washed dishes in Lochboisdale Hotel during my first long break and that was a most forgettable experience. So I decided to try for something on the mainland at the end of the second year. Some of the girls were applying for jobs at Butlins holiday camp in Ayr, so Pat and I decided to fill in a form, as it all sounded quite glamorous. We did get jobs, but they weren't at all glamorous. Pat, poor girl, worked in the kitchens preparing vegetables, while I waited on tables in the dining hall.

It was very hard work, and although all the amenities laid on for the guests were available to us free of charge, we were nearly always too tired to do much at the end of our working day. Once I got used to the running around and learning to carry five plates on one arm and three on the other and being nice to guests when they were obnoxious, the waitressing bit was fun. I was only ever rude to one person while I was there, and I chose a good one.

The incident took place when a young man walked into the dining hall at the end of a long hard day and helped himself to some teaspoons off a table, which I had just set for the next day's breakfast. Teaspoons for some reason were always in very short supply there, and we waitresses guarded them carefully. The Blue Coats, as the supervisors were called, always inspected the tables before each sitting commenced and would dock our wages if there was anything amiss. I called after the young man and told him to "Steal your spoons from someone else, the mean devils who own this place don't give us enough to go round, and then fine us if our tables are short of cutlery."

He just kept going, but about half an hour later a tissue-wrapped package was delivered to me: six teaspoons with a little card on which was written, "Sorry! Won't do it again. Bobby Butlin."

At the end of each week the tips were very good, and when we got a bit more hardened to the job we used to work overtime in the "Pig and Whistle" bar. That was good fun but also hard on the feet. It was the era of "Hi De Hi!" and people really seemed to enjoy themselves at Butlins. I suppose I was lucky to be working in the dining hall and have close contact with the guests, so it wasn't too difficult to enter into the holiday spirit and forget about my aching feet; after all, the smile was as much part of my uniform as the apron.

Pat didn't fare so well, as she had a really disgusting chef to work for and ate hardly anything during the six weeks we were there. She told me tales of maggots being taken out of fish, which was then battered and fried, and the chef's special way of testing the fat, by spitting in it. Apparently his way of cooling off was to sit down in front of the fridge, open the door, take his shoes and socks off and stick his sweaty feet in amongst the food on the refrigerator shelves. We both lost a lot of weight at Butlins and it wasn't all due to the exercise.

We went to a few good parties and saw a lot of celebrities, who were there as part of the entertainment team, and I was offered a Blue Coat's job if I wanted to sign up for the next season. I had already decided that once was enough, however, so I wasn't tempted, and the most lasting memory I have of the place is that of my feet jumping up and down in bed at night when I was trying to get to sleep so that I'd be up the next morning in time to put in an hour's work before the campers were awakened by the tannoy blaring "When it's wet it's fine at Butlins". We were able to save a nice bit of money and appreciate student life a lot more when the next term began.

Pat and I kept in touch for about a year, but she got married fairly soon after leaving college and our lives drifted apart. After all, she was still living in the big city and running around after buses every day, and I was listening to stories about an *each-uisge*. I thought that she was unwise to tie herself down in marriage so soon after what I considered to be the beginning of her own independent life. Now I realise that as she and David, her husband, had been childhood sweethearts, an early marriage was what they had planned. Although married women were actively discouraged from trying to continue their careers at that time, there was always a teacher shortage in the cities, and if she so wished, she'd probably be able to continue with her work. Now I am very glad that she didn't waste time, as she died not too many years into her marriage. Knowing Pat, I'm sure that she had packed everything she wanted to do into her short life.

At the time of Pat's marriage I was very content to be back in South Uist, with a lovely little school, interesting friends and a very full life. It was a life in which, although a boyfriend was always a feature, marriage was something very much consigned to the distant future, way beyond things like getting a car and learning to drive it, passing my probation and going to Canada, and deciding what to wear to the next dance.

CHAPTER
SIX

Keeping up with fashion was a terribly difficult chore if you lived in South Uist at the end of the 1950s, until, like the Magi from the East, came the Indian packmen. It was long before racism was invented, and as far as I know islanders are colour-blind to this day in their attitude to incomers. The packmen were given such a warm welcome that their association with the island still goes on, and at least one of their number settled in Uist, got a job and raised a family there.

They were nearly all called Ali or Malik, but this was no problem, as most of the island families had at least two Donalds and probably a few boys called Angus as well in their own households, having coped with this over the years by using a second name or adding some descriptive prefix. They used the same system to identify the packmen: Tall Ali was Ali *Mòr* (Big Ali), while his shorter fellow-countryman was known as Ali *Beag* (Little Ali). They came to the islands from Glasgow where the goods were made (probably in a sweat shop, but we asked no questions) and toured the villages in vans. The stock was geared to the needs of an island where Willie Jordan and mail order were your sole means of acquiring anything which couldn't be eaten or used to put up a fence.

I remember my mother positively crooning over a plastic tablecloth, and my own joy after mentioning how difficult it was to buy stiff petticoats, so essential for the finished look of the short, full-skirted, glazed cotton dresses that were popular at the time, when Ali — *Beag* or *Mòr*, I can't remember which — went out to his van and brought in an armful of them. Whatever you wanted, they either had it, could bring it next time or, if it was an emergency they could phone the Glasgow factory and have it delivered.

It was extremely difficult to set up any kind of new business on the island, as there were many laws and restrictions. After all, the islands were still owned by a syndicate of people who were really concerned only with running them as a place where the wild and beautiful scenery attracted the shooting and fishing set, and young women wanting stiff petticoats were very low on their list of priorities.

Strangely enough, Willie Jordan, who had been our sole purveyor of clothing for so many years, didn't seem to resent this competitive invasion at all. In fact, I saw him buying a couple of ties once from one of the Indians, while regaling them with stories of his own early days in the business. Although they spoke perfect English, I doubt if they understood half of Willie's stories, but they were much too well-mannered to let him know that.

I wonder what they really thought of the place and its people. As they knew mainland attitudes to be rather less cordial to door-to-door salesmen, going to islands where they were greeted as old friends in every house, and urged to sit down and have something to eat before transacting a substantial bit of business, must have been the realisation of a packman's dream. They showed photographs of their families and spoke of the countries which they had left behind in coming to Britain to seek their fortunes, and send money back for their children. Come to think of it, many of our own young men were sailing off to foreign countries to make money for their families, and here were other families from foreign lands doing the same.

Our neighbour John and many people like him were always glad to see Ali or Malik, as they were a welcome diversion in a hard-working, relatively lonely situation. Once John brought my mother a pile of new tea towels that he didn't need. He said that every time the packmen came he bought some, as he didn't really need any of their stuff and couldn't think of anything else to buy. His towel drawer was getting so full that he couldn't close it any more, so would she do him a favour and use some of them before the packmen came back? My mother said that he should just tell them that he didn't need anything and he replied: "I feel so sorry for them. It's a terrible job for a man going around the country selling knickers."

John's own life was far from easy and his home devoid of luxury, but to him there were more important things in life than the quest for riches.

Attitudes towards people of a different colour were very relaxed, but unfortunately there were other areas that were still prone to a great deal of discrimination. Being a single mother at that time bore a dreadful stigma, as did marrying out of your religion; cohabiting was unheard of and gays stayed well hidden in the closet. If you hit the jackpot and married someone of another religion while in the early stages of pregnancy, it could change your life forever. A father could meet the ferry at Lochboisdale pier and tell his pregnant daughter and her new husband to get back where they came from and stay there. It happened; I knew the girl. It still makes me angry. To me that had nothing to do with Christianity or morality — it was an exercise in bigoted fanaticism.

I suppose things had improved since the real old days when a single woman who had borne a child had to crawl on her knees from the church door to the altar and beg forgiveness of the priest and congregation before being allowed to attend the services again. Still, that happened long ago, even before my mother's time, and as a prehistoric form of birth control I suppose it worked. Strange how the men were not required to take part in this public humiliation, but then I don't think I want to go down that road. Suffice it to say that in Uist, at least in the early part of the decade, the liberated sexy sixties was an era that was happening somewhere else.

Liberated is not the word I would apply to one situation in my memory of that time. I saw a young woman from the next village change overnight from a confident, independent, bubbly person, living and working away from home although still on the island, into a jobless, cowering drudge living with her parents and frightened to death that her baby's cries would bring another rebuke. The first time she went out in public I had been at their house admiring the baby and she walked part of the way home with me. Some people were coming in the opposite direction, and as they approached she took my arm and I could feel that she was literally shaking at the thought of having to face them. She survived, as people do, and married the father of her child, but I ask myself if there had been any productive point at all to the anguish she'd had to suffer after the birth of her firstborn, a joyful if stressful time in any woman's life. I suppose it was an example of humanity being sacrificed on the altar of island distaste for "causing talk".

This profound respect for public opinion caused a lot of friction between my mother and myself on numerous occasions, but never more so than in the case of Jack Dolan. He was a young man from Glasgow who had been a boyfriend and dancing partner towards the end of my time at college. We still wrote to each other regularly when I first moved up to Uist, but we had soon realised that the distance between us was an insurmountable obstacle to any lasting commitment. He always wanted to see the islands and wrote to ask me if he could come up for a week. This engendered a panic in my mother worthy of an imminent German invasion during wartime. Jack automatically assumed that he could stay at our house, and as his family had always made me welcome, I felt that this was quite in order, but my mother would have none of it. "What will people think if you have a man here in the same house?"

Eventually I managed to overcome her objections and Jack came to visit. He was made welcome and greatly enjoyed the Hebrides, even walking across the hill to Glendale and charming the MacIntyres. When he left, my mother — probably influenced by the fact of his being not only a good Catholic but a chartered accountant as well — pronounced him excellent son-in-law material. Unfortunately, I had been totally put off forever when the smart young man-about-town I had been used to seeing in Glasgow came off the ferry wearing a flat cap and a hairy tweed coat. Whoever had advised him on suitable attire for visiting an island had done his romantic ambitions no favours. We parted as friends but my mother was very disappointed. Shortly after my twenty-first birthday she had told me that playing the field was all very well but I'd be a lonely old woman in my old age if I didn't watch out. She had six of us to worry about, so it was a full-time job. The others were no longer within nagging distance, so I came in for more than my fair share of homilies.

The dances, which I have already mentioned, were a weekly or sometimes twice-weekly occurrence. There were several halls by now on the island and the Balivanich Gym, which was a legacy from "airmen" days, was always a very popular venue. Ian MacLaughlin, one of the best accordionists who ever picked up a "squeeze box", lived in Benbecula and played at the Gym. It was he who composed the tune known now as "The Dark Island" and he had been playing the accordion and violin since he was a child. Another talented musician, Duncan MacLellan, lived in Kyles Flodda and he also played for dances. As the dances were all reels and waltzes with the exception of a few quicksteps, accordion music was ideal.

Although there was always some kind of refreshment available in the back rooms of the halls, the beverages were strictly non-alcoholic. You could have cups of tea, sandwiches and so on, served by the tea ladies, and sometimes they had soft drinks and crisps which they sold on behalf of the local shops, but as obtaining a liquor licence was necessary if they wished to serve anything more potent, it was left to people to make their own arrangements in that department.

This usually meant that some young men who needed Dutch courage before asking the ladies to dance with them took a half-bottle of whisky with them and disappeared outside from time to time with their friends to have a wee drink. Some women, too, had their own portable bar with a more ladylike quarter-bottle in their handbag. If all this sounds a bit sordid, just think of the many substances being smoked, injected and sniffed by our contemporaries in other parts of the country at that time. A quarter-bottle between four or five does not a Bacchanalian orgy make.

The Gym has painful memories for my young brother Donald, as it was there that he attended his first dance in his mid-teens. He had saved up and bought a nice suit and a new pair of shoes for the occasion. Unlike the casual attire worn by today's youth when going for a night out, our young men really dressed up for dances, and although they took their jackets off when the temperature in the hall made it necessary, their appearance at the beginning of the night would not disgrace a business convention.

Donald had high hopes of his first dance and had talked about nothing else for weeks. The suit was tried on with various shirts, and as we waited for the dance bus I felt proud of the handsome young man that my little brother had become. He was with a group of friends, and once the long journey to Benbecula was over and the dance started I was too busy enjoying myself to think about him. It was not until near the end of the evening that I realised that I had not seen him since we were on the bus, but the hall had been pretty packed that night and I thought that I had just overlooked him. I saw him sitting at the back of the bus on the way home and it was not until we got off by our house that I noticed anything amiss — as he squelched his way to the door.

The Gym was built on an area of low ground and a large drainage ditch had been dug around it to prevent flooding. In the dark, poor Donald in his new clothes had found this ditch on his way from the bus into the hall and had walked straight over the edge, ending up covered in brown sludge up to his shoulders. He had not even seen the inside of the hall but had spent the evening in the bus, waiting for the dance to finish. His new shoes survived, but the suit, especially after he'd tried to wash it in the kitchen sink before going to bed, was history. We laughed about it later, but as an entry into society, even on an island, it was a disaster of major proportions for a young man.

The mud bath didn't put Donald off dances, and I have memories of sitting in our kitchen after a dance, eating something which he had fried for us and talking about events of the evening until my father came and growled us off to bed. We were young and could survive on very little sleep, but my father always liked a good night's rest before a working day.

The Alginate Industries Factory in Boisdale was where my father had worked since it had been built, first as a casual worker cutting and transporting the seaweed from the shoreline to the factory; at the same time he kept the croft going, as this was still in full swing. For some years now he had been on the permanent staff at Alignate and so had run down the stock to make the croft more manageable. He had worked himself up to foreman at the factory, sometimes doing the manager's job, but was more than happy to put in a day's work with the other local men. Colonel Charles Cameron of Lochiel — known to us all as "an Camshronach" (the Cameron) — owned the factory and from the first day he met my father he took to him and soon began dropping in to our house.

Colonel Cameron did not actually take up residence on the island, but stayed at Lochboisdale Hotel when he visited Uist and spent some time making sure that all was well at his factory. Many an evening he came to our house and sometimes brought other aristocratic friends, such as Viscount Fincastle, whom we knew simply as Johnny Fincastle, to meet my father and talk the evening away. When an Camshronach got married my parents were invited to the wedding, a lavish society affair on the mainland. My mother didn't want to go, but my father went and thoroughly enjoyed it. Most of the time the evening conversations would take the familiar road of folklore and talk of old times. If there was a dram about, my father would sing a few songs and Johnny would also oblige, usually with a ballad called "My Pair of Nicky Tams". It was written in broad Scots and, although we had difficulty understanding the words, being more familiar with pure English, he had a pleasant voice and accompanied the singing with funny actions.

The only time there was any discord was when the talk turned to politics. My father was a very staunch supporter of the Labour Party, as he considered that everything beneficial the islanders had ever received had come through our Labour MP. Charles Cameron came from a long line of Scottish clan chieftains and his political views were not of the working class. A lot of what my father said was purely for effect, but I could see that Charles Cameron took him seriously and got quite angry and I wondered if it was a wise move to antagonise one's boss in this way. My father assured me that for all his aristocratic lineage an Camshronach was a good sport and liked a lively argument.

Apart from the work engendered by the factory, there was little else in the way of job opportunities at our end of the island at that time. There were the roadmen who literally made a lifetime career of maintaining our roads. They were a gang of workers whose lack of speed was legendary, and gave rise to the saying that if you looked out of a plane flying over the island and saw something moving, it could be anything at all but not a roadman.

An egg-packing station opened in Lochboisdale and some people were employed there grading and packing the eggs. It caused a brief flurry of industry, and most of the Kilpheder housewives had crates of day-old chicks sent from the mainland and made a bit of money when the chickens matured and started to lay their eggs. The enterprise flopped and the packing station was closed and re-opened as The Outer Isles Crofters Shop, which was a most welcome establishment, as it was the closest thing to a much needed draper's shop on the island. There was some work to be had in the hotels and shops and also the schools and hospital, but there was still a constant exodus of young people going off to the mainland to seek work.

The tweed industry has had a foothold in the islands since time immemorial, and much of island folklore has been kept alive in the old waulking songs. These were songs sung to help women "waulking" or shrinking the tweed by banging it on a wooden table, to keep the rhythm going. In my Glendale days there was a tweed mill in Iochdar and some of the south-end men worked there on the looms. There were also some families who were outworkers for the mill. They had their own looms and had the wool delivered and the finished tweed collected by a van from the mill on a weekly basis.

A *breabadair* (weaver) toured the island schools and held evening classes where you could learn the various stages that cloth went through from sheep to shop. The isolated situation of Glendale School was no hindrance to the *breabadair's* devotion to the ancient craft, and every autumn he would arrive there with a large loom, several small handlooms, carding paddles, a couple of spinning wheels, bags of wool and anything else he needed to conduct his weaving classes in the school. Neil Campbell transported it all from Ludag to Glendale in his boat and the MacIntyres had another lodger for a couple of weeks. The *breabadair* had been doing his rounds for many years and they knew each other well. Now old age was approaching and he feared that nobody else would want to take on the job when he retired, as it was a demanding task heaving all the equipment about in addition to needing knowledge and skill to teach the craft.

He talked about the history of weaving and how Harris Tweed was in great demand all over the world, and that our own royal family wore it during their visits to Balmoral. From him I learned that although Harris is part of the Hebrides, the wool from Hebridean sheep is not used for the tweed, as it is too coarse and only suitable for carpets. The wool must be from sheep bred in mainland Scotland, and only the best and finest pure virgin wool is used. At that time, to qualify for the orb stamp which showed that the tweed was genuine, the weaving had to be done on one of the Outer Hebridean islands and it had to be woven by Hebrideans. I don't know if those regulations are still in place but it all sounded very romantic.

All the Glendale villagers attended the weaving class, and as they had all done it before, many scarves and small blankets were produced in a short time. I had never even seen a loom before and was quite fascinated by the whole process; carding was good fun. This was when the wool was combed between two spiky bats ready for spinning. I learned how to make a *rolag* (a little pad of carded sheep's wool), and tease it out with one hand while keeping the tension on the spinning wheel steady with the other and moving my foot up and down on a pedal to keep the wheel spinning. I never quite got all the movements co-ordinated and my finished wool was fat in places and very fine in others, but at least I knew the theory.

When the wool came off the wheel we had to attach two strands to a kind of spindle, which was used to weight the ends. By the wool being flicked between finger and thumb in a winding movement the two strands were wound evenly around each other. Again, the pressure used had to be consistent, as if you wound too fast the finished wool would be too loose to be of any use, and if you went the other way and wound too tightly you could end up with a coil of yarn resembling a corkscrew. The older people made it all look so easy, and even the children, having been attending the classes since they could walk, were proficient. I will draw a veil over my own prowess; at least I had entertainment value.

Weaving on the small looms was not difficult, as all you had to do was learn to thread the wool correctly and keep your tension even as you pulled the horizontal crossbar down to fill up the warp — the vertically threaded wool — with weft, the strands that intersected the warp horizontally. The large loom was a little bit more complicated and produced wide pieces of cloth in a variety of patterns according to the skill of the operator. It involved the use of foot pedals, and I had already learned that my hands and feet weren't too good at co-ordinating their movements, so I learned the theory and left the practical exercises to the skilled weavers of Glendale.

October was one month when I could not go home during the week, as that was the month of the Rosary. Each evening the little school became a chapel as the villagers congregated to say the rosary and sing hymns to Our Lady. I had to lead the prayers and the school children led the singing. I have never been particularly religious, probably as a result of overkill while being brought up by my very religious aunts, but I liked the October evenings, and seeing all members of that isolated little community come together to pray for the rest of the world with genuine devotion was a good experience. Once a month the Eriskay priest came over to say Mass in the school, and that was particularly for the benefit of the older villagers who found going further afield to church arduous. The normal school timetable was suspended on that morning, and while the children sang hymns I took on the role usually served by an altar boy, giving responses and so on. Afterwards the priest would chat to the children and sometimes test them on their knowledge of the catechism and saints' days. So the little school behind the hill was a very valuable part of that little community, and its use for purposes other than academic work had become traditional over the years.

CHAPTER
SEVEN

Is truagh fhèin an-dràsta
Mar thàing an galair ud:
Am machair is gach àite
A b' àbhaist bhith cur thairis leo —
Chan eil an donas earball
Eadar Orasaigh is Gramasdal;
Ach nì an seagal fàs
On bhàsaich an coineanach.

Gur olc an obair-là rinn fear
A thug don àite 'n toiseach e,
Toirt a leithid seo de phian
Do na h-ainmhidhean neoichiontach;
'S cinnteach gum bi mìothlachd
Air Dia ann am Flathanas
Nuair ruigeas e an t — siorrachd
'S a dh'iarras e mathanas.

How sad the situation since
that plague came amongst us:
The machair and the places
that used to be full of them —
The devil a tail is to be seen

between Orosay and Gramsdale;
But the rye will grow up high
since the rabbit has been massacred.

What a bad day's work was done
by the man who imported it,
To give such untold pain
to the innocent creatures;
Surely God in His heaven
will treat him with contempt
When he reaches eternity
and begs to get forgiveness.

These are the first and last verses of a poem my
brother Donald John wrote expressing his views on the
releasing of the myxomatosis virus to cull the rabbit
population of the Uists. In his youth he and his
brothers assisted in a kinder form of reducing the threat
posed to the machair grain crops, but the old dog and
torch method was no longer enough, and so there
began an extermination programme which to my mind
was one of the cruellest forms of death I have ever
witnessed. Even hardened crofters were moved by the
scenes of suffering that they saw, and could hardly bear
to go near the machair until it was all over.

If you didn't have to worry about crop damage it was
easy to be beguiled by the vision of rabbit families
cavorting around their burrows, but they were just
another type of vermin to the folk whose livelihood they
threatened. Even so, the reality of seeing eyeless rabbits
beating themselves against the ground, and tearing

chunks of flesh from their own bodies as they writhed about with heads swollen to the size of footballs, was not easy to stomach. It took a long time to get rid of them all, and throughout that time the stench of death hung around the machair, and you could smell the rotting bodies of rabbits from the dunes when you attended a funeral in Hallin cemetery.

Rabbits are hardy creatures and after a few years they began to appear again, but for a long time they were considered unfit to eat lest traces of the virus might have been passed on. I think there are still some people around who remember the sad sights of the myxomatosis days and I hope that when the time comes for another cull the methods used are more humane. Nature is in itself a cruel thing and I don't suppose the rabbits enjoyed being hunted very much either, but at least they stood a sporting chance against the dog and torch.

Sadness also touched the MacIntyre family during my last year in Glendale. Flora, the slight figure I had grown used to seeing, running around feeding chickens and doing things around the byre, no matter how early it was when I topped the rise and saw the house and the bay on a Monday morning, was taken ill. She collapsed and was taken to hospital suffering from internal haemorrhaging. As she was stretchered into Neil Campbell's boat her face looked as if were made out of white tissue paper, and it appeared for all the world as if she had already left us.

The house went quiet and Calum took to sitting by the stove looking at his hands and sighing. He seemed to shrink into himself and hardly ate a bite when Kate Ann cooked her usual hearty dinners; when she tried to get him to go out cockling to take his mind off things, he'd say: "Later. There might be word . . ."

I realised that for all his gruff independent bluster when Flora was around, he was lost without his companion of many years. Happily, Flora responded to treatment. A blood transfusion helped her to regain her strength and she was running around the house again in a matter of weeks. Calum didn't make any public fuss of her when she came back, but he started eating and telling his stories again.

Flora was most amused that Norman MacKinnon, a Daliburgh man who had been the blood donor for her transfusion, came from a staunch Protestant family. Just about every time she mentioned him, she'd shut her eyes and say: "And may God bless the good man and reward him for what he did for me."

Now and then if she disagreed with Kate Ann over something she'd laugh and say: "I don't know if I'm right or not, maybe it's just the Protestant in me coming out."

Although religion had always been a dominant force on the islands, and its observance rigidly in place, people of differing creeds lived alongside each other in peace and harmony. It was only in the case of intermarriage and other controversial situations that family disagreements arose.

Life went on as before and Flora returned to full health, then, in what seemed a pitifully short time, fate struck again. Calum collapsed with a stroke, and after a couple of days and nights during which the whole village took turns to sit by his bedside, he died. I was there when he breathed his last and one of his neighbours turned to me and said, "*Gabhaibh a' 'Verse Anamana', a Chiorstaidh*" ("Say the 'Soul Verse', Christina"). This was a traditional prayer, said on behalf of a dying person at the point of death, asking for the soul's safe conduct out of this world. I put my finger on Calum's cold lips and recited the ancient prayer, and I couldn't believe that I was actually doing this for Calum, my dear old friend. It was a dark period in the house by the bay. It didn't seem possible that life could be so cruel to two of the nicest people I had ever met. At the age of twenty-one I still had a lot to learn.

Despite looking as if a strong breeze could blow her away, Flora had always had a core of steel and, although obviously devastated, bore her loss with calm dignity. She had seen her daughter, Kate Ann, left a widow with three young children while no more than a girl herself, and had given her comfort and support, which was now being repaid. The house was very quiet for a time and then gradually returned to normal, or at least as normal as any house can be when a loved one has gone forever. They spoke about him often and I really think that helped; just talking about how he'd react to different things that were happening, and reminiscing about funny things he used to say, made his absence that little bit easier to bear.

At school the inspector had made his final intimidating visit, and as he had unbent sufficiently to say "Perhaps we can get you a bit closer to home in your next school", I had the feeling that my parchment (the certificate given at the end of a successful probationary period) was forthcoming and that a transfer was also on the cards. It was a funny system in those days: you didn't have much choice in the matter of schools. You were given a list of vacancies and could apply for them, but at the end of the day the Education Authority decided where you should go and personal preference had little to do with it.

I hoped that my move would be to Daliburgh School, a large school in the next village to Kilpheder. I had attended the junior secondary department as a child, but that little corrugated iron building and the old primary school, an imposing stone-built structure next to it, had been closed for some time. The primary school was used as a council office and the old junior secondary school was now used to store building supplies. The large modern school which replaced the old building, incorporating primary and secondary departments, now stood further south on the Daliburgh-Kilpheder road, next to the old technical school, which had also changed its function and had become part of the school canteen.

Changes were happening very rapidly on the island. Time had stood still for a number of post-war years, but then it was as if the world suddenly decided that the islands could do with an update. The coming of electricity and running water to houses had transformed many lives earlier on, and now most of the little thatched houses stood empty as the new houses were built and crofting, never really a paying proposition, became more of a secondary occupation. Crofts had to be worked to some extent to guarantee tenancy, but a lot of the men found other means of providing the money necessary to exist in an increasingly materialistic environment.

The ever-expanding Army population was making its presence felt and many of the children in Benbecula were adopting English as their language of choice. Soon this spread to the south: you could address a child in Gaelic and be answered in English. Many of our young people found work in some capacity within the far-reaching administration and maintenance structure of the army garrison. Another source of employment round about that period had been the construction of the causeway, joining Gramsdale in Benbecula to Carinish in North Uist, and forming the one long island which the three separate islands have now become.

In 1960 the North Ford Causeway was opened by the Queen Mother and for the first time ever you could drive the seventy-odd miles from Lochmaddy to Ludag. The South Ford that separated South Uist from Benbecula had been bridged in 1942 to facilitate access to the port of Lochboisdale, but for many years North Uist had retained its island status, an unknown section of the universe to many South Uist people, even to those of them who had travelled the world.

Although North Uist had a thriving port in Lochmaddy, access from the Benbecula side, even as far as Grimsay, was arduous. You could see it but you could only get there with difficulty. Even at low tide, the North Ford was intimidating and full of quicksands which could swallow an unwary horse and rider in minutes if they strayed off the cairn-marked route. There were two routes you could take; the one which led on to the Ford at Uachdar and wound its way round the north end of Sùnamul to be joined by the second route, which started from Gramsdale and then curved its way round islets to the east before coming back to the west and ending up in Carinish Bay.

I remember my father telling me a story that he had heard in his young days. A man from Benbecula, a priest or doctor, I can't remember which, had been out on a sick call to Carinish late at night. Although it was night time there was a full moon and he decided to risk crossing the Ford, as the tide was still low. The moonlight completely changed the appearance of the Ford, and as it cast shimmers and shadows over the sand and rocks, the man lost his way. The quicksands claimed his horse and trap, and he himself was washed away by the incoming tide. Somehow he managed to swim to one of the small islands and was rescued the next day by fishermen, but such had been his terror that, although he was a young man, his hair had turned completely white.

As soon as the causeway opened, a tour bus from the south started going to Lochmaddy on Sundays and many people went to take a look at this island that they had not seen before. They were probably surprised to find that it did not differ from their own island in many respects, but were interested to see the villages that had only been unfamiliar names to them before the opening of the causeway. One of the North Uist hotels provided a comfort and refreshment stop, and as the people on the bus were classed as bona fide travellers, drinks were available.

There was a story going the rounds at the time that some of the North Uist people objected to people from the Papist south coming to disturb the peace of their strict Sabbath observance, especially as drink was involved. It is said that some families closed their curtains when they saw the bus approaching. I don't know if the story is true or not; my own experiences of the people of North Uist, gained at concerts and dances, were all very cordial.

When A.A. McGregor wrote of the possibility that one day the islands would be joined together, he had said that he couldn't imagine that the islanders would benefit in any way. Well, I think that he's been proven wrong. Having the dangerous fords bridged has brought benefits aplenty to all the islands concerned; not only has it cut down on accidents and loss of life through drowning, but ease of transportation, tourism, the opening up of hitherto isolated communities, the benefit to businesses and the intermingling of three separate cultures have been some of the good results of this difficult but very worthwhile undertaking.

We young people were very pleased to have a whole new community of our peers coming to our dances and found no difficulty in travelling the long distance to *their* dances, over the causeway. I must admit that Lochmaddy was a bit too far away for me, but the village hall at Carinish brings back many memories.

Although better roads and more money brought more cars, most of us young people could still not afford to run one, and although boys with cars were always the most popular, the bulk of the dance-going generation depended on a bus. There were bus services that ran during the day. MacBraynes ran buses to Benbecula geared to connect with the plane and ferry services, but the buses that served the more rural routes and did dance runs were from Fraser MacDonald's fleet in Howmore. Fraser was the son of A.C. MacDonald, the merchant who had a shop in Daliburgh and whose family have carried on the tradition over the years. He had married the daughter of another businessman from further north and had started his own shop, transport and garage business, and it was one of his buses that we used on dance nights.

Angus, who was Fraser's bus driver, knew us all and, although not a dancer himself, he could always be prevailed upon to do a dance run no matter how tired he was after all his normal day's driving duties. He would go out to Lochboisdale and wait until the young people had had a few drinks in the hotel and then drive along to Daliburgh crossroads picking up more people there, then on along through the townships, picking up as he went along, over the causeway and up (or down, as we used to say) north to Benbecula.

It was always a very merry bus as we sang our way to the dance. Old traditional songs were followed by pop songs of the era and we didn't feel the time passing. The journey to Benbecula usually took a little over an hour, and longer if we were going to Carinish. As some of the young men might have been drinking beer in the hotel, they might require a comfort stop, which Angus was willing to provide at a convenient rock or hillock. Once, he caught a group of young men relieving themselves against the back of the bus and he drove off and left them, forcing them to do a very hasty covering-up operation as the people on the back seat jeered and catcalled at them. He was very good-natured but he did have his standards.

His busy working day caught up with him once we got to the hall and he would sleep on the back seat until we came out again. This seemed to be enough rest for him to feel sufficiently refreshed for the long drive back, but one night our merry little gang had a near-death experience in the dance bus.

We had been to the Balivanich Gym and it had been an excellent evening, as usual starting late and going on into the small hours of the morning. We noticed nothing amiss with Angus as we boarded the bus and settled down to sleep the miles away. Angus always remembered where everyone lived and would stop the bus and call out to wake you up when he got to your stop. About halfway home the bus came over the top of a rise in the road: the wheels turned to negotiate a bend but didn't turn back when the road straightened out. In the quiet bus full of sleeping passengers, while watching the wipers clear the windscreen of drizzle, Angus had fallen asleep at the wheel.

The first inkling I had that all was not well was when there was an almighty crashing noise as the bus hit a telegraph pole and snapped it in half. Glass showered in from the broken windscreen and the bus came to a halt in a semi-vertical position with its back-end up in the air. After the initial shocked silence all the lights went out and everybody started screaming at the same time. There was a mad scramble to get out, resulting in a jam about the middle of the bus, as the people at the front seemed reluctant to move. I put on my best teacher manner and called out, "There's no need to panic, take your time and we'll all get off safely."

Then I noticed the water creeping up about my feet. Angus had driven the bus into a loch. I have always had an almost pathological fear of drowning and I thought that my time had come. I am ashamed to admit that the calm person urging the rest of the people not to panic disappeared, and I think I stepped on my sister's head and walked on water to do it, but I was one of the first people off that bus and scrambling up the bank on to the road.

We all lost our handbags and other things, which were on seats and on the floor, as the bus was almost totally submerged before long, but had Angus been driving at a greater speed, or had the pole not slowed the bus down, we could have easily lost our lives. There are some who say that Angus was drunk, but my own opinion, for what it's worth, is that he was simply worn out with tiredness and that in a way we who were always urging him to do dance runs for us were as much to blame for the accident as he was.

Alternative transport was summoned to take us home, and although we were cold, wet and covered in diesel and mud, miraculously nobody was hurt. My father had scant sympathy for us and told us that he was sure we'd be off to a dance on the moon if there was a bus going there the next night. The same old routine started as soon as Angus got another bus, so perhaps my father was right.

Shortly after that, my brother Donald and I pooled our resources to buy a car. It was a green Morris Traveller, the kind with wooden bits all round it, of the type which is now a cherished vintage classic, but to us it was our key to independent motoring — if only one of us could pass our test. It used to belong to Theresa MacPhee, who was our next-door neighbour's daughter, so we were confident that it was a good buy. The registration number was PUS 85, and although I have had many cars over the years and would be hard-pressed to tell you the registration number of the current one, I'll never forget PUS. Why do I remember it so well? The first time Donald drove it he ran over my sister's cat.

It was not as heartless as it sounds. Most of the Hebridean dogs, cats and sheep of the time were on a constant suicide mission. Dogs considered that cars were there to chase, while the cats were very fond of falling asleep under a car and, becoming confused on waking, would dart out in front of a wheel. Sheep were fairly sensible, unless one of their lambs was on the far side of the road, when the mothering instinct could make them rush across to defend it. So learning to drive in South Uist at that time was quite an adventure.

Donald had been driving various vehicles since he was old enough to climb on to a tractor, and apart from the cat he had a clean record, even if he hadn't bothered with the formality of applying for a provisional driving licence. The police on the island at the time were fairly lenient, but once a matter was brought to their attention they had to act on it. In other words, if you didn't cause any problems with your car and nobody reported you, the road was yours as long as you could get away with it. The driving test was only held once a year, as examiners came from the mainland to conduct it. They had to fail a certain quota each time and were pretty terrified of Uist roads themselves, so getting a licence was a long hard slog.

I think Donald eventually took his test in London, where, with very little instruction, he passed first time, but while he drove PUS he did so while playing cat and mouse with the South Uist police. One night he was outside one of the dance halls and was just locking the car when he saw the two Lochboisdale policemen walking up. He dropped his keys on the ground and called to them, "Am I glad to see you! I've just dropped the keys to this car and my friend, the driver, will be very angry if I don't find them. Could you please shine your torch down here for a minute?"

The policemen got down on their hands and knees and found the keys for him. Handing them back to him, they said, "There you are, sir. Look after them now!"

Donald was not known to the police, so he got away with it for a long time and eventually left the island still without a driving licence. I was more conventional and went through the proper channels. The Highway Code book became my Bible as I struggled with motorway lane procedure, right-of-way on a roundabout and other facts of driving life which, although I could learn them, I would not be able to practise on single-track roads, where the main hazard was a maternally inclined sheep. My father tried to give me driving lessons, but his instincts for self-preservation were strong. As he had never sat a driving test but had been presented with a licence to drive everything under the sun during the war, so that he could drive the Ministry of Agriculture's tractor in the village, he was not really the right person to cope with my nervous attempts.

I had a few lessons with other drivers and applied for my driving test. I failed it, of course. I thought that I should have passed and couldn't agree that I had reversed on to the wrong side of a road when the road in question was only marginally wider than the car in the first place. The examiner was writing my Fail report as he asked me the Highway Code questions, so I didn't even try to give sensible answers. The worst thing about my driving test failure was that it was actually documented in a published book, for anyone who could afford 18 shillings to read it. I refer to *Scotch on the Rocks* by Arthur Swinson, Chapter 3, page 80: after describing his first meeting with my father, the author goes on to say

His elder daughter was quite depressed, having failed her driving test that afternoon, so we spent a few moments commiserating with her about the finer points of the Highway Code.

It wasn't the Highway Code that had caused my failure. I just wasn't anywhere near confident enough to drive, and would have been a danger to myself and others if I had passed, but with the arrogance of youth I wasn't ready to admit that.

The great day dawned, my parchment arrived and I was free of probationary status. In the same post came a letter confirming my appointment to the staff of Daliburgh Primary School, and so I said a final farewell to the little community living around Glendale Bay. The life skills which I had been privileged to acquire while teaching and living there have stood me in good stead over the years, and there was no inspection or certificate for those. Nowadays, young teachers have mentors to guide them through their first few years. I could have asked for no better mentors and educators in every aspect of life, and even death itself, than the MacIntyre family of Bay View, South Glendale. They are all gone now, but I am sure that many of the teachers who spent time with them share my views.

CHAPTER
EIGHT

It had been a year of enlightenment for my father. Not only had he crossed the causeway to North Uist, but also in the same year he actually crossed the Border and took his first real peek over Hadrian's Wall as a tourist, when he went down to England to attend Donald John and Brenda's wedding in the Hampshire village of Eweshott. He had rushed down to England once before, to the Liverpool area when Donald Angus was hospitalised there, but grief and worry had occupied his mind and he spent most of the time in and out of hospitals, so he could remember few details about the place.

His croft work and the factory had left little time for travel in previous years, although he knew Glasgow well, as he went there frequently to work with the BBC and the School of Scottish Studies. England was a place that he often reviled as a country where men ran baths for their wives and crept around their own homes in aprons, although he had little first-hand knowledge of the country or its people. His view, often shared by people who have never travelled, is that if you haven't been there it couldn't possibly be worth visiting anyway. Scotland and especially the islands were Utopia as far as he was concerned.

The reason for his and other people of his generation's antipathy towards the English goes back to their history lessons in school, where they learned that as far back as they could care to remember they would find the English committing dastardly deeds against the Scots. My father could quote them all: there was Edward I, the Hammer of the Scots, who gave Wallace and Bruce much grief, and then came his son Edward II, the very first Prince of Wales, who also tried to tame the Scots and got his come-uppance at the Battle of Bannockburn. When his wife Isabella had him brought to a sticky end in Berkeley Castle, along came the next Edward. What was his first outing after his coronation? A nice trip to Halidon Hill to knock seven bells out of the Scots. On and on my father would drone: the first Queen Elizabeth dealt very badly with Mary, Queen of Scots, and so on. From Tin Hat Cromwell to Butcher Cumberland, leaping out from the pages of his school history book and enshrined forever in his amazing memory, there they all were, with most of them clutching a severed Scot's head in their fist. Not exactly the best basis for good cross-border relations. However, as far as his own family marrying the enemy was concerned, he agreed to keep an open mind, as he had no option.

My mother, my father and I went to Donald John's wedding together. I was to be bridesmaid and, as it was such a special occasion, we splashed out and travelled to Glasgow by plane. This was another new experience for him, as had always shunned air travel even when the BBC paid his expenses, preferring the boat and train journey. He would say, "I'm not afraid of flying, just afraid of dying. If anything happens to the boat I can swim, but if anything happens to the plane I can't fly."

Fortunately, his first flight was a short turbulence-free experience, and although he clutched the arm rests and went white when the plane revved up on the runway, he soon relaxed.

Seen from the air for the first time, the Uists can make you wonder how people can survive amongst so much water. If the Earth from space looks like a blue planet, then the Uists from the air look like a blue island interspersed with specks of brown land. As the winding ribbon of road running from north to south disappeared under a cloud, my father turned to me and said, "If we crash now, the swimming will still come in handy."

Looking out of the window until the tiny little dot that was Canna disappeared soon took his mind off the miles of fresh air between him and the ground, and when we landed at the old Renfrew Airport, he was amazed that the journey had taken so little time. From that moment on he was a confirmed flyer and the BBC had to provide for an airfare in his expenses from then on.

The long train journey down to England was a source of great interest to my father, as he marvelled at the neat green fields with their tidy brown and white cows, all looking as if some sculptor had placed them

114

there. He kept saying, "It all looks so well scrubbed. Is the whole of England as clean as this?"

It was my own first trip across the Border, so I couldn't give him an answer. I realised that he was worried about the impression he was going to make on his son's future in-laws when he said, "What will they make of my hands?"

My father had large square hands and, although he was very particular cleaning them, his hard work over the years was reflected in the scars and callouses on his palms. My mother by this time was getting nervous herself, so she snapped at him, "I'll knit you a pair of gloves and you can wear them all the time you're there if you're so vain."

The whole wedding episode went very well, with Brenda's family and ours forging a lasting friendship and, although they owned a substantial part of Eweshott, they were no strangers to hard work. So my father's misgivings about their reaction to a working man's hands were unfounded, and he spent much time talking about different breeds of cows and things like that with Brenda's Uncle Ed, a man whose hands showed a remarkable similarity to his own.

The wedding itself went off without a hitch, although when Susie Cranstone, the other bridesmaid, and I went back to the house to change out of our finery into more casual wear for the evening dance we found that neither of us had brought a key. There was a bathroom window open, and we ended up climbing a ladder and squeezing in through the little window in our beautiful bridesmaids' dresses.

On his return home my father was full of praise for England, but of course there was the odd barb as well: "When they offer you a cup of tea that's all they're offering. You get a cup of tea, no scone, no sandwich, no oatcake, no nothing. Imagine! Just a cup of bad tea!"

He liked his tea strong and practically stewed and served as a mere accompaniment to a substantial plate of goodies. Donald John and Brenda spent their honeymoon in Uist and we saw the other side of the coin when she'd been taken on the usual tour of friends and relatives. After the obligatory cup of tea with all the trimmings in every house, she declared that she would never eat again.

Donald Angus also married his English girl that year, in London, but it was a small quiet wedding as he'd just spent time in hospital with a stomach ulcer. We didn't manage to attend the wedding, but when he brought Sheila home she and my father got on very well, and although he would still poke fun at the English and call my mother "dahling" in an affected English voice from time to time, I think his association with some of the nicer members of the country made him view England in a better light.

After the summer holidays I started working at Daliburgh School, and it was a strange experience sharing a staffroom with some of the teachers who had taught me in my own schooldays, in the not too distant past. It must have been a bit strange for them too, but they didn't seem to mind and were very good colleagues. One of my old secondary teachers lost track of time one day and called out to me to stop running in the corridor. We laughed about it afterwards and the easy camaraderie that developed between us made me forget about the old days when she had not been my favourite teacher.

"Porky", as we used to call her, was from another island and had often been the butt of practical jokes and pranks played on her by the little beasts we were in those days, in the old corrugated-iron school by the loch. During that time we had not made her life easy and she retaliated by using her belt quite frequently. Fortunately her aim was bad and she often missed most of your hand. The more she lost her temper, the wilder her aim became, and I remember going home one day with the imprint of the Lochgelly's three fingers all the way up my arm.

On that particular day long ago, she had been supervising two classes, as the teacher in the classroom next door had to go home because of illness. The Headmaster asked her to leave the connecting door open and set the other class some work, as it was near the end of the morning, and he'd take the class himself in the afternoon. When she had done a bit of teaching with her own class, she went into the room next door and came back with a white face, as there wasn't a single child to be seen. The other classroom was completely empty and it had no outside door, so she couldn't figure out where the children had got to. She looked very worried.

Worry changed to anger, however, when the lost children entered her classroom through the outside door, filing solemnly past her, the boys saluting and the girls bowing their heads as they each bade her "Good morning, Miss" and, going silently through to their own room, sat down at their desks. They had all jumped out of the window, then closed it after them, and had walked round the school and back in, to give her a fright. Her own class was delighted with this diversion and shouted with laughter. The belt was well used that morning, and as I was in her class and my two older brothers in the pranksters' class and she punished us all, the MacMillans scored a hat-trick that day.

Fortunately, none of my pupils at the new Daliburgh Primary School tried any tricks like that on me, and although I had a class of Top Juniors larger than the entire number of pupils at my previous school, we got on well together. Not having been an angel myself during my schooldays actually helped, as I could spot trouble coming a mile away and take steps to avert it. I had to call "Porky" by her Christian name when we met in the staffroom and, as she was a nice gentle person in real life, I felt quite sorry for the trouble she'd had to put up with in the old days.

Now that I was living at home, it was easier to get on with my driving lessons. My closest friend was Jean, daughter of A.C. Macdonald, and when we weren't doing anything else I'd pick her up in PUS and we'd drive all over the island. She had been driving since she was old enough to take her test and as an instructor she was the best. If she ever felt any panic, she never showed it, and that built up my confidence.

On a fine Saturday we would drive out to isolated parts of the island to avoid traffic and practise hill-starts and emergency stops and all that. The long winding road out to Loch Skipport was a favourite route, and when the rhododendrons were in bloom we'd pick bunches of them to bring home. If we were lucky, when we reached the end of the road and stopped to give the Highway Code a going over, we could park on the old pier and watch porpoises at play out in the harbour.

During this time A.C. or Ailean Mòr (Big Alan), as he was known, was in poor health. He was getting on in years and his declining health forced him to leave the running of the business to his son and daughters, and spend most of his time sitting around the house. When Jean and I had finished our driving I'd go in with her to have a cup of tea and A.C. would come into the kitchen to enquire about our progress. I got to see another side of the aloof astute business image he had always presented to his customers and remember him as a very nice person full of local knowledge and always glad of a chance to talk.

My parents had always thought highly of him and his wife since the time when, as a teenaged naval apprentice, my brother Donald Angus had the dreadful accident which cost him his hand. My father left home immediately to be with his injured son, but first he had to go to A.C.'s shop to buy a new suitcase, as the ones we had at home were all falling to bits. It was a Sunday when we got the news and my father was very apologetic as he asked A.C. if he would open the shop and sell him a bag. Not only did he open the shop, but he and his wife filled the suitcase with everything my father would require for his journey and food for the family. When he tried to pay for it all, they would not accept a penny in payment.

Having heard about. A.C.'s generosity in our time of need, I wasn't at all surprised to find that he was such a human person, but I was very impressed by his deep knowledge of the island and its history. From him I learned that the pier we used as our pit stop in Loch Skipport had been built by Lady Gordon Cathcart in the 1870s and that at the time there had been whispers that she'd had it built, not for the purpose of bringing in supplies to the island, but to make it easier to ship emigrants out. He also told me about the history of Lochboisdale Hotel and that it had been a much larger building when it was built in the reign of Queen Victoria, until fire had destroyed part of it a few years after the end of the First World War, and that the new building was therefore not as large as the old one. We heard the story about the building of Daliburgh Hospital, and although I'd heard it before from my Auntie Chirsty, Alan gave it a different flavour and I didn't mind hearing it again.

Many were the war stories he told us, having lived through two world wars. It chilled my blood to hear how the Highland Pipers were always the first on to a battlefield, on the assumption that the weird noise of the pipes might strike terror into the enemy, and remind their own ranks that they were fighting for Scotland as well as England. As a weapon the pipes

120

were not too effective and the band was often decimated. Alan shook his head sadly as he told us that the drummer boy, never more than a schoolboy, was nearly always killed. Many of the pipers came from the Highlands and Islands and he could recite lists of young men who left home proudly and came back in a box or not at all.

From Lochmaddy or Loch nam Madadh (Loch of the Hounds), which he told us was named for watchdogs and had been a port where pirates used to congregate in the seventeenth century, through Benbecula and all the way to the Standing Stones at Pollachar, he had a rich fund of stories and information to which we would listen while the cups of tea by our elbows went cold.

There were many old people like Alan in Uist at that time, people who had had many experiences of life on the island and elsewhere. They had many stories and would tell them to anybody who wanted to listen, as their knowledge of folklore was immense. Writers, mostly from the mainland, who would come to the island for a few days and record or write notes, and then go away and write a book, often tapped this fund. Although he himself often helped people with their research, my father deplored the situation and expressed a wish that "someone should tell our story from the inside".

He was a great admirer of Margaret Fay Shaw, who had spent some years in South Lochboisdale gathering folklore and actually living with the people about whom she was writing.

He also got on well with Arthur Swinson, who, although not only an incomer but an Englishman, spent much time at our house recording stories and facts about the wreck of the *Politician*. It was he who included my driving test failure in his book, but apart from that he was a nice man. A veteran of the infantry, having served in India, Burma and Malaya, Arthur would sometimes be telling the stories instead of recording them. He had several plays and books to his credit at that time and was just finishing a long association with the BBC as a producer and writer; he was an accomplished man who felt quite at home in our crofthouse. We eagerly awaited the publication of his book and knew that he would not "rubbish" the island.

I was still planning to go over to Canada to teach once I'd done a year at my new school, and I asked the headmaster if he could advise me on the best way to go about it. He was quite enthusiastic and said that, as long as I could promise him a year's unbroken service, he would be happy to arrange a teacher exchange with the Canadian government. The Teacher-Exchange programme had just started and I think that he was quite excited at the thought of having a Canadian at Daliburgh School. We would each teach at the other's school for two years and then swap back again.

It all seemed very simple, but when I mentioned this to my friend Mary Dalzell from college days, with whom I was still in close touch, she told me not to do it. She knew Glasgow teachers who had gone over as part of the exchange programme and they had not been very happy. The teacher was paid by the Education Authority in her own country and also paid tax at that country's rate. The cost of living in Canada at that time was very high and teachers were highly paid to compensate for that. Canadian taxation was low, so the Canadian teachers coming over were well pleased with their lot, while British teachers had a struggle trying to make ends meet, trying to balance a low British salary against the high cost of Canadian living.

Armed with this knowledge, I decided that I would emigrate for a couple of years and see how it went. If I did that, at least I would be paid the same as Canadian teachers. I made enquiries and established that there would be no problems with this plan, and my tentative enquiries about jobs in Canada got very encouraging replies. I would have to spend at least three months in Glasgow when the time came, sorting out all the paper-work, and then I'd be on my way.

Meanwhile, I still had to complete my year at Daliburgh and the headmaster asked me if I would add another term to that and leave at the following Christmas holidays, so that the new Top Junior class could be settled in by a teacher already familiar with the school. So, with much time still in hand before having to start the preparations, I got on with life and pushed Canada to the back of my mind, feeling that I had done well getting it all planned well in advance.

Although there was still some time to go before the next driving tests, I kept up the lessons, and as always there was plenty going on in the evenings. There was a spate of Beauty Queen competitions and these usually took place at dances. I had no ambitions in that direction myself, especially as I was as blind as a bat without my glasses and I had never seen a bespectacled Beauty Queen, but Jean was a very pretty, tall, slim, blue-eyed blonde and had once won the Cameron Queen competition, an annual event held by the Queen's Own Cameron Highlanders, at a dance on Benbecula, so we went to most of the Beauty Queen dances and I rooted for her. There were a lot of pretty blonde blue-eyed girls around at that time, and as far as I can recall she did not repeat her success, but we enjoyed the dances anyway.

The way the contests were run was a bit strange. The girls couldn't enter their names and be eliminated, as happens in other contests I had seen. (At Butlins we used to have a queen chosen every week and the prestigious Miss United Kingdom competition, with the winner automatically qualifying for an entry into the Miss World competition, was staged there.) In the Gym all the would-be contestants were asked to take the floor with their partners and dance an elimination dance, while the judges walked amongst the dancers, giving some girls a ticket. If you were given a ticket, you left the floor when the music stopped. So it went on until only one couple was left and the lucky female was then pronounced as Queen of the May, or Cameron Queen, or whatever. I suppose it beats the swimsuit parade, but to my mind being given a ticket and told to leave the floor must have been the equivalent of "Hop it, you're ugly!" Horrible.

There were weekly dances at the Sergeants' Mess in Balivanich and we went there from time to time. The Officers' Mess also had functions but less frequently, and they tended to be strictly Invitation Only evenings. I had cousins in Benbecula who invited me to stay now and then, and we'd go to the Mess if there was something going on. I enjoyed it, but was a bit wary of any soldiers showing an interest in me, as I always had a sneaking suspicion that there might be a lonely wife looking after some children in some other country. Homegrown talent was fine by me: it was easier to check out.

CHAPTER
NINE

The Aunties, my foster parents for many of my childhood years, had left Barra while I was at college. They were getting close to retirement age, so the teacher auntie Catherine took an assistant's post at Garrynamonie School; they both wanted to spend their retirement years in Uist and they considered that it would be easier to make their plans if they were actually on the right island when the time came to set up their own home. Although Aunt Catherine was no longer a headteacher, as she had been at all her previous schools, accommodation came with the job, and by the time I came back to Uist they had been in their little house for some time.

Before each college autumn term started we had to do a three-week course of practical work, teaching and observing at one of our local schools, and I had chosen Garrynamonie School for my practice ground one year, actually teaching and observing in the same classroom as my auntie. This was a strange situation for me, and I think we both felt a bit awkward teaching in the same room. However, I learned a lot from her and she gave me some sound advice. Although I still felt very much a child when she was around, we both survived the experience.

Garrynamonie School was familiar territory to Auntie Catherine, as she had attended it as a child and had gone on to become a pupil teacher there before leaving the island for Glasgow to complete her training at Notre Dame Training College. It was a strange twist of fate that she should end her career where it had all begun, so many years ago. Frederick Rea, author of *A School in South Uist*, had been her headmaster when she first taught there as a student, and whenever I pick up the book in which he describes his time there, I see her pretty young face on the cover standing next to the great Rea himself, darkeyed and earnest, looking for all the world like a more serious version of my own daughter.

During my teaching years on the island I often visited the aunties in their little schoolhouse and I heard many tales that Aunt Catherine remembered from her earlier time at the school. Apart from the hen story which I have already related, there were many more about her pupils. However, I was more interested in the changes in attitude in the workplace between the current time and the days when Aunt Catherine first started out. I had noticed the extremely deferential attitude she adopted when addressing the headmaster of Garrynamonie School and realised that this was a consequence of the island perception of people in authority that had prevailed in her young days. In those days the headmaster was only marginally less powerful than God. The idea of any kind of equality between the sexes had never been heard of and would have raised a good laugh if it had.

In the Garrynamonie School of Aunt Catherine's young days, when she had attended as a pupil, there was no National Dried Milk being served, and certainly no school dinners. The children often took a hot potato to school in their pocket and warmed their hands on it until they ate it at playtime. The peat fires in the classroom had to be fed too, and each child was supposed to bring a peat to school each day to supplement the school peat. Sometimes a family couldn't spare any peat, or a child would forget to bring it, so some of the children worked out a strategy to avoid censure.

The "peatless" child would stand outside the building, under the classroom window which was next to the peat box, and wait. Meanwhile, in the classroom, when the teacher had her back turned, another child would go to the peat box and, on the pretext of stoking the fire, would open the window to let the draught fan the flames. He would take a peat and throw it out of the window to his waiting classmate. The child could then come into the classroom, apologise for being late, and put "his" peat in the box. I could see that even in those far off days a canny child could be a match for any teacher.

The aunties continued their love-hate relationship with my father. He, poor man, did his best to be a good brother-in-law, helping them with their moves and trying to keep his temper under control when Auntie Chirsty referred to his home as "the house that should have been mine". To her he was still the incomer from Benbecula who had taken her croft. The feud went on till the very end, with my mother doing a constant peacekeeping job worthy of the UN.

As retirement approached, Auntie Chirsty kept dropping hints that she would like our old thatched croft house renovated for their retirement cottage, but, fortunately for my father's sanity, they got one of the newly built pensioners' bungalows on the Daliburgh — Lochboisdale road instead. They moved in and lived there for many years.

I have always considered it a great pity that Aunty Chirsty had never allowed herself to get to know my father properly. She had kept her resentment against him alive all her life, and yet, had she allowed it to happen, I'm sure that they could have become friends. Not as serious as her sister, she had a wicked sense of humour which he appreciated and they both loved songs and stories; in fact, they had much in common and it was an opportunity wasted. Land disputes have caused many family rifts on the island, even though much of the land is still only held in tenancy.

Religious bigotry, also the cause of many a war, has always been my own pet hate. As far as I'm concerned, we are all trying to get to the same place and how we travel there and whether we choose a leader to follow is a matter of choice for the individual. One of the instances of this nasty curse against God and humanity in which I happened to be personally involved took place during the time when I was teaching at Daliburgh School.

The parish priest had asked me if I would consider helping to organise a Youth Club with some other members of the parish, and I agreed. We were always organising concerts and dances in St Peter's Hall anyway and it seemed a good idea. It was the largest hall in the area, and when we talked about it we decided that we could start off a drama group and a country dancing class, some piping classes and other activities, without any problems. We needed some props for the drama group and records for the country dancing and a few other things, so we decided to hold a small *Cèilidh Cruinn* in the hall to raise funds. *Cèilidh Cruinn*, literally translated as Round Ceilidh, was a very informal type of concert where the audience and performers were not segregated but sat in a circle round the hall. It was easy to organise, and you could start off with only a few performers and pick out people from the audience to contribute songs and poems as the evening went along.

We had a very good evening and raised a fair sum of money. Before the people left we announced that the new Youth Club would be starting on the following Wednesday and that all young people would be welcome to attend. Many of the younger ones stayed behind to ask questions and get further details. A girl from Daliburgh had come to the ceilidh and had sung some songs. She had a lovely voice and we all enjoyed her performance. Before she left I asked her if she was interested in joining the Youth Club and helping us to form a small choir. She said that she'd love to, as she lived near the church and, there being no young people of her own age living near her, it got a bit lonely at times.

When the hall had cleared and we were ready to lock up I was chatting to the priest, and he mentioned how much he had enjoyed the girl's singing, so I told him that I had already asked her to join the Youth Club. I was horrified at his reaction.

"You must tell her that you made a mistake," he said. "She can't join. This is a Catholic Youth Club and she's a Protestant."

I was really shocked and angry, but I had to comply with his wishes. She was very good about it and said, "Don't worry about it, the minister's just as bad." At that moment I felt like being very rude to him and leaving him to run his own club, but I didn't want to let the others down, so I held my tongue.

I am not decrying any religion, but that priest's interpretation of Christianity, at least on that occasion, just didn't tie up with the things I had heard about previous priests who had lived in that house and had given their lives to improve the lot of *all* the islanders. Not only Father Allan McDonald, who had worked himself to death, but his successor Father George Rigg, another true Christian who had caught typhoid while nursing a sick family and had died after four years in the parish, still a young man. I doubt if the policy of exclusion had any place in their dealings with the people. I know that discrimination can be found in many places but sometimes you are made aware of it only when it touches your own life.

The Youth Club started and it was much enjoyed by all involved in it, as there was little else in the way of organised activities available to the younger teenagers at the time. The various classes were a way of keeping the island tradition of music alive, and we were fortunate to have a great piper, Pipe Major John MacDonald, living in retirement next door to the church. He was only too pleased to give piping lessons to the youngsters and would stay on to watch the country dancing and other activities.

There were only a few television sets on the island at the time and reception was poor. If we wanted to travel to Benbecula, we could go to the cinema in the Army camp and watch films in comfort, but our own local arrangements for seeing films were still locked in the dark ages of the church hall, hard wooden chairs, a portable screen and a projector which frequently broke down. There was always a break in the story when the reels had to be changed, and if something went wrong with the projector the heroine would suddenly start talking in a deep gruff voice.

The old ceilidhs where people from your village came to your house in winter and sang and told stories were already dying out. People say that TV killed the ceilidh culture, but I think that its demise started when the thatched houses gave way to the modern ones and the cosy atmosphere with its black stove and Tilley lamp went with them. In the old days croft work used to be relaxed in winter, and this meant that the families could sit up late and have a lie-in in the mornings. As more crofters got day jobs and had to be up early to get to their place of work, the difference between summer and winter habits diminished and the ceilidhs gradually stopped.

We still had the Games days and Sales days and there was a fair amount of jollification at New Year, but nothing like the protracted celebrations of my childhood. People stayed closer to home and families tended to have their own little parties much the same way as their counterparts on the mainland. The old ways had already begun to give way to a new order. The travelling shop came to your door if you didn't want to walk to Daliburgh to do your shopping, and life in general was easier for the housewife.

John and Hector, our neighbours and my father's lifelong friends, came to see us from time to time, but Hector was no longer a bachelor and his new responsibilities kept him closer to home. When he did visit he seemed to spend his time talking about sheep and cows and the new "buck rake", whatever that was. John had health problems and tried to stop drinking altogether, but now and then he would break out and nearly always end up at our house afterwards. Whether it was the absence of his sidekick Hector or not I don't know, but now and again he'd end up in some strange situation, ranging from sleeping in the wrong house to getting arrested. He mistook our old house for his own on one occasion and spent the night there. The fact that the thatched roof was half gone and most of the floor space taken up by sacks of potatoes must have alerted him to his mistake, but by then he couldn't summon the energy to go home and he slept among the potatoes till morning.

One morning he called in to our house looking very dishevelled and white-faced, informing us that he now had a police record. My parents were very surprised, as we all knew that, although he didn't take as much care of himself as he should, there wasn't a criminal bone in his body. So he told us of the events of the previous day. He had heard that the Outer Isles Crofters Shop had some good shoes for sale, and as his Sunday ones were past their best, he'd cycled out to Lochboisdale when he'd finished his afternoon chores and bought a nice pair of black brogues.

Just as he was about to set off homewards, he met an old friend who persuaded him to go up the brae to the Lochboisdale hotel for a pint. As time passed he discovered many old friends, and by the time he got on his bike to come back home he was feeling no pain. He made a few attempts to ride his bike, steering with one hand while holding the shoebox tucked under his arm in the other, but before he got very far he realised that he was practically going round in circles. So he got off the bike, discarded the shoebox and, after tying the laces together, he slung the shoes round his neck and got back on the bike. This was much better, and with two hands now free for steering he pedalled his slightly erratic way homewards along the dark Lochboisdale road.

The dynamo light on his bike needed some stronger pedal power than John in his inebriated state could supply, so it just flickered about, but he got along fine until he saw a car approaching at some speed. On pulling over to the side of the road, he felt the front wheel skidding on a pile of gravel left there by the roadmen and he went head over handlebars into the ditch.

As ill luck would have it, the oncoming car was the Lochboisdale police car, and when the driver saw the bicycle lying on the gravel with its wheels still spinning, he stopped to investigate. The occupants of the car were not our usual policemen, who had grown used to the custom of sometimes turning a blind eye, but two young mainland policemen who were relieving them over the holiday period, and as they helped John out of the ditch and on to his feet one of them exclaimed: "You've been drinking. I can smell it!"

Scenting danger, John turned round sharply to deny the charge, and as he did so one of the shoes, still slung around his neck, whizzed round and hit the policeman in the eye! Thinking that he had been assaulted, the policeman and his colleague bundled John and his bike into the back of the police car and without further ado took him to the police station, where he had spent a soggy, frightened night in the cells.

In the morning the policemen decided to drop the charges after hearing John's explanation and abject apologies, and he was let off with a caution. John was much chastened and vowed never to touch another drop — and we all said, "Till next time".

One of his main fears was that his escapade would be reported in the newspapers, but as I was the local reporter for the *Oban Times* and *Stornoway Gazette* at the time, I was able to reassure him on that score. Maybe I should have teased him a little, but I didn't have the heart for it; he had suffered enough.

John carried on dropping in occasionally, and if other members of his family were home from the mainland, they would all come over to our house and we would have a ceilidh, just like the old days. Sometimes we'd also have visitors from Canada, Australia and New Zealand, people whose ancestors had been born in Uist and had emigrated, by choice or otherwise. Most of our visitors had traced their roots back to the island and had some connection to our family, either through blood or friendship. As I have found out myself, wherever you are in the world, if you are an Islander, "home" means your native isle, so these people came to see the place which their ancestors had spoken of and sung about and had always called "home".

Many of the Scots-Canadian visitors were proud to demonstrate that they could make themselves understood in Gaelic and they told us that the original emigrants had kept the language and culture alive through the generations in many parts of the country. There were Gaelic Societies and piping competitions in many of the provinces, particularly in Vancouver and Nova Scotia, they said. They advised me to forget about Nova Scotia for my own plans, as the climate in winter was very tough, and they said that I should try for Vancouver instead as it had a more temperate climate and exiled Scots and their descendants made up a large percentage of the population. They also said that it would be easy for me to get a good job there, as

Scottish-trained teachers were very highly thought of, and that if I needed a sponsor they would speak for me.

At school we had a new member of staff, an art teacher from Kirkcudbright in the south of Scotland. Dorothy was about my age, the only child of a middle-class mainland family, and although it was her first experience of living on an island she quickly settled in. Soon she was going to dances on the bus with Jean and myself and becoming involved in all aspects of the local social life. Although she loved the island and her art, she really hated teaching; her favourite saying was "Teaching would be just great if it wasn't for the blasted kids."

I don't know what the problem was, but I do know that if you don't at least like children, teaching must be torture, as they can smell the fear a mile away and make your life even more miserable. However, Dorothy decided to give it a year and then try for something else. Meanwhile, she concentrated on all the entertainment that Uist had to offer and joined Jean in her efforts to persuade me to abandon my plans for leaving the island. Jean always changed the subject when I mentioned Canada, and although I insisted that I was only going for two years or so and would be back, she'd say: "Don't you believe it, you'll be married to a Mountie and living in a log cabin eating maple syrup with everything before you know it."

I wasn't in the least bit interested in anyone in uniform on the island, unlike Dorothy, who had a soldier boyfriend, and Jean, who was being romanced by one of our young policemen, so I'd point this out to her, but she still didn't like the idea of my leaving. Jean's own future was very much tied up with the family business and she was quite content with that.

Dorothy soon became familiar with the various families and learned not to talk too much about her pupils in a staffroom where you could be talking in derogatory terms about a child and one of your colleagues would say, "He's my nephew".

But even with her improved knowledge she sometimes made mistakes. One day she was talking about a child in one of her classes who had a pronounced Glasgow accent and one of the other teachers said, "That'll be one of the Homers."

Later that day Dorothy remarked to the teacher in question that the child was not a Homer, as there was no family with that surname on her register. She didn't know that this was the collective label given to the many children from the Homes who were fostered by island parents.

I don't know when the policy of bringing groups of mainland children to the island and dishing them out to any family who volunteered to give them a home started. As there were many Homers of my parents' ages around, I suppose it had been in place since before the Second World War, if not even earlier. By my time the regulations had been tightened up but the Homer tag still remained. The children seemed happy enough, becoming members of their new families very quickly, learning the language and helping out around the crofts of their foster families. They were soon accepted by their peers and didn't seem to mind being known as

Homers, although, looking back, it wasn't very politically correct. I've often heard the children introducing themselves to someone and adding "I'm a Homer". They didn't appear to consider the term demeaning in any way. Many of them made the island their home and few went back to their birth families, but some went the way of the island youth, leaving to work on the mainland when they left school. In the days when they were brought to the island and offered around to whoever wanted them, it must have been a really traumatic experience for them, but it all seemed to work out all right in the end. They were brought up in good caring homes and I never heard of any being sent back.

In the spring of my year at Daliburgh School, the annual driving test loomed up again. I was desperately anxious to pass so that I could have a little experience of driving my car before it fell to pieces from old age. The police were getting more careful about checking licences, and as I knew them personally there was a strong chance of my being caught if I took the risk of driving by myself. When the time came, I took the test and passed it, but to this day I'm not quite sure if I did so on my own merits or not. I do know that on the evening before the test, several brawny young men of my acquaintance sought the examiner out in the hotel bar and treated him to a few drinks. They mentioned that a friend of theirs was taking her test the next day and that they hoped she was going to pass it.

The next day in Lochboisdale, just before I got into the car to start my test drive, these young men turned up, greeting the examiner and wishing me luck, and they were leaning against the wall of The Outer Isles Crofters Shop when we returned to do the final Highway Code test. They folded their arms across their chests and stared at Mr Veitch, the examiner, when he produced the pink Fail slips and the green Pass slips. When he started writing on the much-valued piece of green paper, they applauded loudly and I was not the only one who looked relieved. I had nothing to do with that exercise and was quite annoyed when they told me about the drinking session the night before. Perhaps I would have passed anyway — Jean's tuition would have seen to that — and as I have been driving for many years in many countries without ever causing an accident, I don't think that the intimidation of the examiner, if that is what was intended, had been necessary.

There was much jubilation that night and we had an invitation to a party at the police station. I have a hazy recollection of being locked in one of the cells for refusing to drink a vile concoction that someone had mixed for me, and thinking that I'd hate to spend time in that dark damp smelly place. The party continued at Jean's house until dawn, when we got Ian, Jean's brother, out of bed to drive us all down to the Kilpheder sands in his big van to watch the sunrise. There was quite a crowd of us, all young people, walking along the white, white sands on a clear early morning watching the sun come up over the horizon and listening to the stillness broken only by the lapping of the waves and the lonely bark of a seal calf from the colony on the rocks in the distance. I remember someone starting to sing "Stranger on the Shore" and Dorothy saying: "If I could paint this, I'd never have to teach another child, ever."

And Ian, ever the voice of reason, shouting at us, "God, you're mad, the lot of you! Get back in the van and I'll take you home, I'm freezing."

When I got up the next morning, my first day as a qualified driver, I couldn't even remember where I had left the car.

CHAPTER
TEN

Auntie Catherine wanted a holiday. She and Auntie Chirsty had moved from the schoolhouse some time previously, on her retirement, and were living in their little pensioners' bungalow in Leonard Place, Daliburgh, and I think she felt that after her long years of teaching she was free to have a bit of fun. So, almost as soon as the boxes were unpacked, she had taken my mother on a pilgrimage. This outing had not been an unqualified success, as my mother got a bad case of food poisoning during the journey to Lourdes, and very nearly reversed the whole Lourdes claim of curing all ills by going there healthy and coming back half-dead.

Now Auntie Catherine wanted me to go to Allington Castle, a Carmelite priory in Aylesham, Kent, and join her on a fortnight's prayer, fasting and retreat holiday. My auntie's capacity for enjoyment knew no bounds. I don't think she was in any way trying to improve my moral welfare; she just didn't want to be on her own, especially with all the Brothers about.

In her later years Auntie Chirsty had developed a tendency to take to her bed frequently and sleep a lot. She called her ailment *an ruaidh* and I have no translation for that — stress, perhaps? Maybe she thought that after her years as her sister's housekeeper and helping to bring up our family, she deserved a bit of mollycoddling, I don't know. It didn't seem to bother Auntie Catherine and, as they were both pretty old, they deserved to live their lives as they wished. She had flatly refused to join Catherine on any of her jaunts and my mother had decided that one brush with death was enough, and in future would confine herself to solo shopping trips to Glasgow, so that's how I became the chosen one.

My summer holidays had already been planned, so I put up quite a struggle. My young sister Mary Flora was working at the Castle Rock Hotel in Woolacombe, Devon, and I wanted to go down there to see her and have a proper resort holiday at the same time. My two brothers Donald Angus and Donald John and their wives had produced baby daughters, so a visit to London *en route* was also a possibility. When Auntie approached me with her request I was less than enthusiastic; at first I flatly refused, but she looked so disappointed and there were a lot of "You wouldn't be where you are today . . ." comments coming from Auntie Chirsty's bedroom, so eventually I gave in.

Much haggling ensued, and eventually we agreed that we would go to London to see the babies for a few days, then on to Aylesford for a week. She could retreat and fast as much as she liked, but I would just have a quiet holiday, "forgetting the cares of the outside world, watching the swans on the moat and reading in the tranquil garden." (This alternative to the holy holiday was also offered in the brochure.) Then we'd go on to

Devon, where Auntie Catherine could read in a tranquil garden while I would join my sister in a kind of anti-retreat. My father found endless amusement in this unlikely pairing of holiday companions, but as it turned out it was a very enjoyable trip.

The little ones, Catherine and Kay, were very sweet and our time in London too short, although Sheila took us to see the sights and Auntie loved St Paul's and the Brompton Oratory. We had a picnic in St James's Park and fed the ducks by the pond; outside Buckingham Palace she echoed many people's reservations about the need of one family for so many imposing residences, but, being a genuinely humble person all her life, she qualified the observation by saying "But it is not for the likes of us to find fault with the likes of them."

It was good to see my two older brothers again and to see that they were well and happy. As always, they were hungry for news of the island and we spent much time talking and laughing about the old days. Donald John showed me his latest songs and poems and I was pleased to see that he didn't let his busy life interfere with his talent. Brenda told me that she was always finding bits of paper around the house covered in his writing and she had learnt not to throw anything out if it was written in Gaelic. Although he lived and worked in London, he always wrote about Uist and events that took place there, and always in Gaelic. I think his writing was a kind of antidote to the city and the often stressful work of a policeman.

Leaving London, we took the train through the lush summer countryside of Kent to Aylesford. Brenda and

Sheila decided to come with us, and they brought the little girls, who charmed everyone near us on the train. They had heard of the Carmelite priory, but until now had not visited it and were eager to know what it was like inside. Aunt Catherine phoned ahead and booked them in to have their evening meal with us before returning home.

Allington Castle was very interesting, imposing and mediaeval-looking from the outside. Inside the old moated castle a hooded monk showed us to a room devoid of all luxury, with the original stone walls unadorned by any form of concession to the twentieth century, and I must say that I had misgivings at first. There were two narrow wooden beds, flanked by washstands, each with a basin and a jug on top, and I thought "I've been here before"; it looked like a more austere version of the Convent.

Sheila was horrified at the starkness of it all, and Brenda said, "I suppose they are trying to keep everything authentic."

They stayed for the evening meal, which was very palatable, but as all the guests sat at an enormous refectory table and a monk said a ten-minute grace before we could eat, then proceeded to sit at the top of the table throughout the meal, conversation was stilted. When Brenda and Sheila were taking leave of us with their babes, Sheila whispered in my ear:

"Listen, girl, if you get desperate, send up a smoke signal and we'll come and break you out." She was an ex-WREN, so I suppose it looked a bit like a prison to her, but to me, an ex-convent girl, it didn't look so bad.

I spent the week watching a pair of swans building their nest on a little island in the moat and did a lot of reading in gardens that were tranquil indeed. Although I took no part in imposed silences or fasting, sometimes the beautiful plainsong hymns drew me into the chapel and I shall always remember that week as an oasis of calm in a life which I thought I had planned to perfection but which, unbeknown to me at the time, was about to spin well out of its intended orbit.

Devon was great. I saw a lot of my sister, Mary Flora, and as we had seen very little of each other hitherto, with me being at home while she was with the aunties, her being back home when I was in Glasgow and Fort William, and then my living at home and teaching locally when she had left, it was good to make a start on getting to know each other. In later years we discovered many common interests and parallels in our tastes, such as liking the same books and enjoying the outdoors. For sisters, having no childhood baggage probably helps, and we get along very well.

There were other island girls working at the Castle Rock Hotel, including the daughter of Mary by the Canal, the dear departed old friend of my childhood days, and the week just flew by. We talked, went to Ilfracombe to see the donkeys, were invited to a beach barbecue and did touristy things.

Auntie Catherine didn't go too far from the hotel, as she was scandalised by the sight of all the young people in shorts and swimsuits walking around, or, as she described them, "Half-naked folk. Have they no shame?"

146

Still, she enjoyed sitting in the sun and talking to some other silver-haired residents who were intrigued by her accent. I'm sure that when she returned to Auntie Chirsty she probably told her that Mary Flora was working in a place that was a cross between Sodom and Gomorrah.

On the way back we stopped off in Glasgow to see Alick, and he seemed to be getting on well with his plants and things and had a good circle of friends, so we could give my parents a favourable report on all their far-flung children. I took the opportunity to meet with the Director of Education at Glasgow Corporation headquarters, to ask about the possibility of employment while I was tying up the paperwork for Canada. He immediately offered me a job at St Jude's Primary School in Barlanark, as a teacher at that school was retiring and about to start her final term.

Before I left the Director's office I had signed a contract to start there at the beginning of the following January. He understood that I was only going to be in Glasgow until my emigration papers and passport business was sorted out, so he said that we could review the situation at the end of my first term. I was well pleased and on my return to Uist I sent off a letter to Inverness Education Authority giving them a term's notice.

Now that it was all beginning to look real, my parents were sighing a little as they watched me start to sort things out in my room and put things to one side for packing, but they had grown used to seeing their children going off to work elsewhere, so they didn't put up any objections. My mother had given up her crusade to get me to "settle down", and as my longest running romance had been with a boy from North Uist and it had raised a bit of the old religious controversy, I think she may have been secretly relieved when that ended. I must admit that the thought of all the raised eyebrows on both sides of the North Ford probably kept that association going longer than it might have done otherwise, but it was fun while it lasted.

Dorothy had given up on the teaching profession and was pursuing an application to join Pan American Airways as a hostess. She was accepted almost immediately and was also working a term's notice at Daliburgh School. There we got our classes ready for handing over to our successors, who had already been appointed. The Youth Club was still going strong, and although I had started to drop out of the concert circuit, I went when I had the time. We still went to dances with Jean and the gang and it was all going along just fine, until one night at a dance in the Balivanich Gym when I did something totally out of character and gave the time of day to an English soldier, a REME Warrant Officer. Three weeks later I was engaged to him. Canadian plans went out of the window, at least for the moment, and the future was nothing if not uncertain. As our Ruby Wedding approaches, neither of us can explain how two sane people could have reached such an important decision so rapidly and why it should have happened at that time in our lives, but whatever the reason, we are not sorry that it did.

Love at first sight? No way. We spent our first evening together having a huge argument, and when he asked if he could see me again, my answer was "Not if I see you first."

He was very persistent, however, and, as you can gather, things improved between us. Colin had been in Benbecula for three years and was due for posting out in a few months, but our paths had never crossed; I was just about to leave the island for Glasgow and then move on to Canada, and now this had happened. It was all very inconvenient. My parents took it all in their stride and were quite taken with Colin when they met him, although my father gave him a grilling worthy of any Victorian patriarch and then told me: "He'll do, but are you sure that he's not too sensible for you?"

My mother was all pleased and twittery about planning a wedding. She liked Colin but I have the sneaking suspicion that she would have embraced Willie Jordan as a son-in-law if it made me "stop gallivanting and behave like a proper teacher".

I was never sure what that meant, but I think it involved wearing a fur coat and a hat to church and praying a lot.

Jean was delighted and Dorothy claimed some responsibility, as she had mentioned Colin to me several times and had actually introduced us. However neither of them could see how it was all going to end, as I was working my final month of notice at Daliburgh and there was a teacher's desk in Barlanark, many miles of land and sea away, with my name on it. With the mad optimism of youth, I was sure that we could work things out as we went along — after all, my long-term planning had not exactly proved foolproof.

There was a lot of toing and froing between Benbecula and Kilpheder as Colin got to know my family and friends. It wasn't too easy for him, as he had no car of his own and had to rely on the generosity of car-owning friends. When the friends were using their cars themselves, one of the Benbecula shopkeepers, Charlie MacLeod, a friend of both my parents with whom Colin was acquainted, told him to borrow his van whenever he liked. Charlie had been one of my mother's admirers in her carefree single days while she had been living with Aunt Catherine in Benbecula. He was happy to be involved in the present turn of events and seldom used the van in the evening himself, as he was getting on in years.

Colin's journeys from Benbecula to Kilpheder went smoothly as a rule, but once or twice he found out that sheep were not the only hazard on island roads. One evening he was coming down fairly late and it was already dark when he picked up the keys and thanked Charlie.

"Watch out for the dog, now," said Charlie.

As Colin manoeuvred the van out of its tight parking space between the shop and a stone wall he kept a sharp lookout through the windscreen, in case he should run the dog over. He couldn't see any sign of the animal and, putting the gear into reverse, he looked over his shoulder. As he did so two bright eyes looked straight into his and a wet tongue slathered its way from his forehead to his chin. Charlie's dog had been

150

sleeping on the back seat of the van. Charlie came running out when he heard the van crashing into the wall, but as there was no lasting damage to wall, vehicle, driver or furry passenger, all he said was "I'm sorry, Colin, I should have told you he was sleeping in the van."

I expect the story went down well in the bar of Creagorry Hotel that night. My father enjoyed it too.

On another night Colin didn't seem to be his usual self, looking preoccupied and being very quiet. Most of the time, if he and my father were in the same room, I couldn't get a word in edgeways and as I had been out when he'd arrived at the house, I thought that they'd had a falling-out over something and left it at that. My father thought that Colin and I had had a disagreement over the phone earlier, and waited for me to come home and hopefully sort things out, as there was a definite atmosphere. When I'd been there for a while and things were still strained, my mother said: "What's up, Colin, aren't you feeling well? You look as if you've seen a ghost."

"I didn't see one," he replied, "but I definitely think I've felt one around me."

When he was driving down the South Uist road, past Beinn na Coraraidh and the big rock that stood there, he felt the hairs on the back of his neck stand up and a cold draught from the back of the car made a shiver go through his whole body. He could feel a presence in the back of the car but was too scared to look in the rear-view mirror. His mind told him to stop the car and investigate, but his body wouldn't obey it and a few minutes later the atmosphere changed back to normal. He stopped and checked the car but there was nothing on the back seat and the windows were closed.

"I felt as if something really evil was in there with me," he said.

He had just passed a big rock. Remember the rock with the crack in it that had featured in Donald the Glendale postman's story? That was the one. Colin swore that he had never heard that story until we told him about it after we'd heard of his experience, and I believed him, as he's not the type to bother making things up for effect. Although he drove home in the dark that night and many other nights, it never happened again.

Our neighbour John was full of misgivings about my taking up with a soldier and told me many dark tales of women who had got into trouble with the servicemen during the war. All left penniless and shoeless, with a houseful of babies, when the rascally airmen went back to their English wives, he said. I don't know where he got his information from, as he had never stirred too far from his croft and I couldn't think of any Kilpheder women fitting his description. When he met the soldier in question, he declared him far too much like an Islander to be an Englishman, let alone a soldier. Praise indeed.

Another fan club started when Colin met the aunties. They had invited us to tea and had bought a new china teaset for the occasion. Now, if you've seen the comedy *Father Ted*, in which the housekeeper's plates of sandwiches are like the Cairngorms, the aunties always produced a table that would make Mrs Doyle's efforts pale into insignificance, and on this occasion they had excelled themselves. Fortunately, Colin has a very good appetite and, being forewarned, had starved himself for most of the day in preparation, so he just ate and ate and ate. The cups of tea kept coming and he kept putting them away. The aunties were mightily impressed. When we were leaving, Auntie Chirsty presented him with a pair of the special socks, grey ones, knitted in the finest soft two-ply wool, which she always made for my brothers. He had eaten his way into her good books on that occasion, but on future visits he had cause to regret his enthusiasm for the table, as the food began to take over most of the room.

At the end of the term and my final days at Daliburgh School I felt very sad. I had loved it there and was sure that no Glasgow school could ever come up to its standards either in terms of friendly staff or well-behaved, bright pupils. Dorothy was also leaving and she, Jean and I had a little "wake" for the days of yore. Jean was a bit brighter about my departure than she had been: first because I wasn't going straight to Canada now, but there was also another reason — one of Colin's army friends, John McDonnell, had expressed an interest in meeting her, and as she had admired him from afar for some time but they both seemed a bit shy about making a move, we thought we'd play Cupid and arrange a foursome. It was an unqualified success and I think they are about three years behind us in their wedding anniversaries. Not as precipitous as our engagement, but Jean came from a canny family.

Talking of families, I still had to meet my prospective in-laws, so after taking leave of Daliburgh School, Colin and I went to Bristol to meet his family and stay for Christmas. From there I would go straight to Glasgow, where I had arranged lodgings with my college friend Mary Dalzell's family. Colin would leave me there with all my worldly goods and continue his journey on to Uist.

We sailed on the *Claymore*, the larger and more stable successor to the awful *Lochness*, but still not a drive-on, drive-off ferry. The cars were driven on to a big net, the driver got out and the net was gathered up and winched on board by a crane. We hadn't brought a car, as I doubt if PUS would have survived the net, let alone the journey. Instead we took the train from Oban to Buchanan Street Station in Glasgow and then transferred to Central Station to catch the Bristol train. We were late getting in to Buchanan Street and didn't have much time in hand before the Bristol train left, so we were not too happy to see the taxi rank completely devoid of taxis. As I was effectively moving house at the end of the holiday, we were loaded down with luggage, and as we puffed our way as fast as we could up the incline towards Central Station, I thought that we were both going to die. We made it to the station, just before the whistle blew, but it was a good ten minutes before either of us could speak.

The visit was good. No strangeness at all right from the moment Colin's mother opened the door, and a little later when he had left the room, she whispered to me: "I've always been afraid that he'd come back from foreign parts with a black wife, it makes it so difficult for the poor children."

So I was of an acceptable colour at least. At that moment she reminded me of my own mother and her strange ways of evaluating people. I loved Bristol: it was such a clean bright city, and although it was a very cold winter with much snow about, we did a lot of sight-seeing. Theatres, cathedrals, docks and the beautiful old university at the top of Park Street, Brunel's station and suspension bridge, the Nails — large metal objects rising from a cobbled square on whose surface the slavers would place their money when a bargain had been struck over some unlucky slave, thus giving rise to the saying "paid on the nail" — so much history held within a few square miles; I liked it all. We also paid a visit to a jeweller's and Colin bought me a lovely diamond ring and I liked that too, and he bought himself a car.

I had my first experience of an English Christmas, which we spent with Colin's brother and his family. Then his mother hired a hall and arranged a huge party where I met what seemed like more relatives than the entire population of South Uist in one evening. All too soon it was time to head north again.

The weather had deteriorated steadily over Christmas and New Year, and the whole country was in the grip of one of the worst winters it had hitherto known. We left early in the morning, and although it had taken us nearly an hour to dig the car out of the snow before we set off, it wasn't too bad once we got onto the major roads. There were no motorways then, so Shap was rather dicey, as a blizzard blew up just as we were approaching the summit. It was a frightful journey from then on: the weather got worse and worse, and after a brief overnight stop and an early start, it was evening of the next day before we made it to Glasgow.

The Dalzell family lived on the borders of Springburn and Balornock in a solid old tenement house which was like a haven of warmth after the howling blizzard and ice storm conditions through which we had been driving for the best part of two days. I was at the end of my journey, but Colin only had time for a hot drink and a sandwich before having to turn the car around and head out of Glasgow towards Oban to catch the boat for Lochboisdale.

I really didn't envy him one bit, and knowing the narrow unlit roads he had to travel once he was out of the city, I was concerned for his safety in the worst driving conditions imaginable. The route from Glasgow to Oban, even in those days long before the construction of the present-day road, was still one of the prettiest in the country. In good weather you drove between towering mountains reflected in clear lochs and a picture postcard view awaited round every bend. In winter darkness, in a blizzard, when one wiper is frozen to the windscreen and the other has been whipped off by the howling wind, it's a different story. I could imagine all sorts of different scenarios, all resulting in my being single again before I'd even got used to the weight of the engagement ring on my finger.

When Colin called me the next evening, I found out that my fears had not been unfounded. It had been a hazardous journey. Under the narrow old roads of the time there were gulleys for drainage to stop the water cascading off the high ground on either side of the roads during rainstorms and causing flooding. The freezing cold wind had iced up the water in the gullies, resulting in a blockage, and the water, then free to gush across the roads, had gradually frozen. The water running down the sides had also frozen and great slabs of ice had fallen on to the road here and there. Not ideal conditions for someone driving that road for the first time, in the dark.

To make matters even worse, the signpost at the Tarbet intersection, which should have pointed him in the right direction for Crianlarich and the turn-off for Oban, had been turned around by the high wind and was pointing to the left instead of the right. Colin had followed this road for half an hour before he stopped at Arrochar to check the map, found out his mistake and had to turn back. Eventually, within sight of Oban, he saw a pub in the distance; hoping that it would still be open and have a bed available, he went up the side road and parked outside. The pub was open, and such was the landlord's astonishment that someone had actually driven from Bristol in that weather that Colin was treated to free drinks all night. He sat there with only the landlord for company till he could summon enough energy to drag himself off to bed for a few hours' sleep, as he had to be up in time for the early morning sailing of the *Claymore*. Back in Balornock, I'd worried for a bit, but Mary and I had much to catch up on and we burned a bit of midnight oil till I started falling asleep in my chair.

CHAPTER
ELEVEN

How do you know when a friendship begins? My first memory of Mary Dalzell is quite clear. We were both in our first year at college and it was the Wednesday morning Speech Class.

I am not quite sure what the purpose of this class was: maybe it was a means of giving us an opportunity to build up our public-speaking skills so that we'd be able to make ourselves heard as we yelled "Put him down!" across a Glasgow playground. We were allocated topics on the spot, and we spoke about them for a couple of minutes. It was torture for some students and they died a thousand deaths while stumbling through some boring little homily on "How to Iron a Shirt" or "My Best Day" with a dry mouth. Any MacMillan can talk for Scotland, so I didn't mind Speech Class at all.

On that particular day I had been given the subject "It Makes My Blood Boil" to talk about, and for my speech I'd chosen to castigate Elizabeth Taylor, who had just stolen Eddie Fisher from cute little Debbie Reynolds, causing her to go into a decline. I had been reading about Ms Taylor in a downmarket rag and my tirade was quite informative. Across the room I caught

Mary's eye. She gave me a wicked grin and pointed to the lecturer, who was hanging on to my every word. She then pointed to the clock and gave me a cautious "thumbs up". The message was implicit: "Keep going as long as you can and it won't get round to my turn."

No problem — when I ran out of facts, I just made it up as I went along and had to conclude after a while, as it was getting tiring. The lecturer only had time to say, "Well, that was different!" before the bell went, and so began a friendship.

At college we didn't really have the exclusive "best friend" kind of relationships that schoolchildren have: you were more likely to be a member of several different groups. There were always one or two people with whom you found more common ground than others, and during the final year you already knew which of the friendships would endure; for me Pat Plunkett and Mary Dalzell fell into this category. Soon after leaving college Pat had married and contact was gradually lost, but wherever Mary and I have been in the world, and although there can be years between meetings, our friendship has spanned the decades and is still strong.

So when I started lodging with the Dalzells during my teaching time in Glasgow I was already familiar with the house and its occupants. Mary's mother was a tall, dark-haired woman with a commanding presence who originally came from Dalry in Ayrshire. Her father was an equally tall, equally dark-haired man from Belfast in Northern Ireland and one whom I always think of as a quiet, very calm man. Mary, their only child, was small and fair-haired, and to my mind bore little resemblance to either of them in looks or manner. She was not as strident as her mother and certainly not as calm as her father, but always either on the brink of gloomy disaster or ecstatic exuberance. I suppose dramatic is the word I'm looking for. It was an interesting household.

Mary had come to Uist with me during one or two breaks and had a dalliance with one of my older brothers for a short while, but it didn't last. She loved the island and all the social life of the time. As she had no brothers or sisters, mixing with our large, diverse, mobile family must have been a novel experience for her, very different to her own ordered existence as a cherished only child. I think her mother considered me as a calming influence on Mary and had always treated me as a second daughter during my college days, so when she invited me to use their spare bedroom during my spell at St Jude's I had no qualms about accepting the offer.

Christmas holidays are short, so I barely had time to sleep the arduous journey from Bristol out of my bones before I was trudging through the snow to the bus stop to catch the first of two buses that would take me to my new school on the outskirts of the city. There had been no time to arrange a preliminary visit, as the school had been closed for the holidays, and in those days there was no such thing as the present-day system of holding in-service training, giving teachers a couple of child-free days to sort things out before the pupils arrive to begin a new term. Then we all arrived together on the first day of term with varying degrees of reluctance.

St Jude's was a very large school and a harassed headmaster greeted me with relief and gratitude. One of his new appointees had not turned up, but had left a note in his mailbox telling him that she had changed her mind and would not be joining his staff, so he was glad to see that he had at least one of his two new teachers on site.

He told me that a large percentage of his pupils came from a vast block of high-rise council flats nearby, into which — and this is a direct quote — "the Corporation decanted the families when they tarted up the Gorbals and Cowcaddens".

Both areas mentioned were slums, so that explained the speed with which I had been offered the job. I wondered if walking through the playground had been enough to make the other incumbent take to her heels. My own ears were still ringing from the ripe language I had heard as I had fought my way through the squabbling crowd to get into the school building, but as at that point at least the children were directing their abuse at each other, I was apprehensive but willing to give it a try. I was a bit concerned, however, when he asked me if I would mind leaving my classroom door open and supervising the teacherless class, which was in the room next to mine, until he could arrange cover. I had a vision of poor old Porky's missing class scenario being re-enacted.

My concern was well justified when I found that I had forty ten-year-olds on my own register and a composite class of forty-two nine- and ten-year-olds next door. How do you teach eighty-two children? There is only one answer: you can't. You can set them lessons and mark their work, but forget any thoughts of getting to know their individual needs. Hearing each child read and helping anyone with difficulties could take the whole school day. It took a month to get a long-term supply teacher in, and my job description for that period could have been written in two words: crowd control. One thing surprised me, however: discipline was not a problem. The children of that time, especially in the poorer areas, still had a healthy respect for authority, and once they came into the school building their teachers' word was law. Marking their work took many hours, but as ignoring the work that a child has struggled to complete is pretty cruel, it took care of many evenings at the Dalzell table.

Mary was teaching at St Aloysius Primary, a Springburn school within walking distance from her home, and we saw little of each other during the week, as our work kept us so busy, and my working day involved so much travelling. She was on the point of becoming engaged herself, to Charles Boyle, a medical student, and when we did have time to talk it was mostly about future hopes and past memories. One memory in particular caused us some amusement, the holiday on the Isle of Man after our graduation.

Mary's mother had bought a raffle ticket at the doctor's surgery where she worked and, as the raffle was for charity and she had never won a prize in her life, she had even not bothered to check the list of prizes on offer. Some weeks later she was delighted to find that she had won a holiday for two on the Isle of Man, which she very generously gave to Mary and myself to celebrate the end of our student days.

We had a wonderful first week, going to see Ivy Benson's All Girl Orchestra who played in the pavilion at the sea front, swimming and sunbathing, sightseeing and shopping. In many ways it was a great week, but on the Friday, with one week to go, we both felt a bit disappointed, as our money was nearly all gone and we hadn't met any boys. The clientele of the boarding house were all blue-rinsed couples and most of the boys we'd seen appeared to be holidaying with their girlfriends. Then, on the Saturday morning, after we'd gone up to our room to get our stuff together for the beach, there was a knock on our bedroom door and there stood two young men with porcelain chamberpots on their heads asking: "Do you have THESE under your beds?"

It's the first and last time that I had ever heard that chat-up line being used. Bob and Hugh were lads from Aberdeen who had checked in that morning, seen us as they were passing through the dining room, and had been trying to work out how to introduce themselves. They were quite mad but they certainly livened up our final week. We were able to show them around, have a lot of laughs and generally have the holiday that we thought we were going to have in the first place. At the end of the week, as they waved us off on the plane, we wondered if any young girls were booking in to our boarding house so that they could model the pots again.

The Glasgow of my teaching days was a million light years away from our present "City of Culture". Then it embraced many cultures, and some of them specialised in the use of razors, so you were careful where you walked after dark. The buildings were tall, gloomy and grimy in many areas, and although the more affluent districts were pleasant, even the snow couldn't improve parts of it. The dreadful winter continued as the snow settled and froze and fresh flurries fell on top of that to become a grey slush as we all slipped and slithered through it, trying to remain upright as best we could. It was dark when I went to catch the bus in the morning, and by the time I got back after school the yellow glow from the streetlamps was again lighting up the gloomy scene. Then I got jaundice, through eating some "iffy" meat dressed up as a curry, and was very ill and pretty yellow myself for two weeks.

When I had recovered and rejoined the staff of St Jude's, the weather had changed for the better and I was able to go out more at weekends. Sometimes I met my brother Alick, who was still working at the Carmunnock nurseries, and we'd have a day out together. I also saw something of my aunt Mary Margaret, my father's sister, who lived with her husband and family in Govanhill. My father came from a large family of seven boys and one girl and, with one exception, Uncle Allan who worked the old family croft in Benbecula, they were scattered about from Glasgow to Fort William, so I never got round them all. There were many ex-Islanders in the city and at my mother's instigation I managed to visit a few of her old friends.

Islanders who lived and worked in Glasgow have always kept up the links with their heritage, and in the early 60s there were many places in the city where they congregated. There were organised groups like the Uist and Barra Association, and one for Mull and Iona etc, where people from specific island groups met and held concerts and dances to keep up their contacts and sustain the Gaelic culture. There were also many meeting places in the city such as the Hielanman's Umbrella and Paisley Road Toll where you could find Islanders talking Gaelic in animated groups, especially after dances in St Margaret's Hall, Kinning Park.

Mary and I had some nights out, dancing at the Highlanders' Institute and Govan Town Hall mainly, but the weather and our respective jobs often made an evening in watching television a more attractive alternative. Mary's father often had meetings in the evenings and her mother would join us to watch *Come Dancing*, her favourite programme. If we wanted a snack before going to bed, we took turns to prepare it, and it soon became apparent that Mrs Dalzell was the only one amongst us who could produce anything half-edible. I couldn't even make something on toast properly. The toast was either burnt or tough and chewy because I had made it too soon and it had time to get cold before I'd made the topping. My scrambled eggs were grey and granular and so rubbery that they refused to stay on the toast.

Mary's mother decided that, as both her daughter and I were in great danger of poisoning our husbands when the time came that we would have to cook for them, we should look for an evening class which would at least teach us how to produce a survival diet. She said: "I know Colin's in the army and he won't be fussy, but there are limits, and Charles will soon be a doctor and he can cure himself, but think of your children."

She herself had a full-time job and had no time to teach us, and anyway she told us that as her own cooking skills had just been picked up as she was growing up, she couldn't teach them to anyone else.

"I just taste it and add a pinch of this and a handful of that."

It was all Greek to us, so we agreed to give the thought of an evening class some consideration. I suppose the fact that we had both gone to schools where you were taught academic subjects to the exclusion of all else, unless you were going to teach home economics or take an Institutional Management course at college, had added to our ignorance. I remember the appetising smells coming out of the Domestic Science building at Fort William School, and I'm sure that none of the pupils in that class needed a crash course in cookery before getting married.

Going back out to be taught something after a day's teaching didn't really appeal to either of us, so in the end it was Mary's mother who phoned around, found a suitable class and enrolled us in it. It was a six-week course and included a bit of basic instruction, but it soon became clear to us that we were the Special Needs pair in the class. We didn't know the difference between short crust and flaky pastry, and had never heard of a roux. The woman taking the class was quite horrified to see Mary banging a ball of pastry on the table and saying, "It's just like playing with plasticine."

"Cool fingers, cool fingers, girls! Good pastry must be cool in the making and hot in the baking!" she exhorted.

I don't know if the instructor was ever the same again after the conclusion of the classes, but at least we managed to produce a meal to take home at the end of the six weeks. It consisted of a vegetable curry and a Swiss apple tart. Mary's curry was better than mine, as I'd let the onions burn, giving the finished dish an interestingly acrid taste, but the meringue on her tart was flat, while mine was fluffy if a bit raw. So we had a very substantial supper that night, and Mr Dalzell suggested that, as our mistakes seemed to cancel each other out, perhaps we should look for houses with an adjoining kitchen when the time came to put our newly acquired skills to the test.

By the time I went home to Uist for the half-term break, I had decided that I would not renew my contract at the end of the term, but would try for a school closer to home. Colin had been sent to the St Kilda outpost of the Guided Weapons Range and so, had I still been in Uist, I wouldn't have seen much of him anyway, and with the primary purpose of moving to Glasgow, namely emigration to Canada, now abandoned, there didn't seem to be any reason for my being there.

I was not at all optimistic about getting appointed to a school on my own island. Most appointments were made at the beginning of the autumn term when the new graduates joined the profession. As the applicants usually outnumbered the posts, a job on your home island was like gold and most teachers held on to theirs pretty firmly. However, I thought that anywhere in the Highlands would at least be closer and certainly more appealing than my current Blackboard Jungle work environment. My job was fine as long as I was within the four walls of the classroom, but playground duty was tough, and patrolling the dining hall during the lunch hour made feeding time at the zoo look like a state banquet.

Letters from my parents and phone calls kept me in touch with the family, and the envelopes with the puffin stamp bearing the logo "St Kilda, the furthest station West" were eagerly awaited. Colin didn't mind the isolation of the St Kilda camp, as he was keenly interested in birds and all kinds of natural history, and spent a lot of his spare time taking photographs of the wildlife. The island's social history also fascinated him, as many of the buildings used by the inhabitants before they were evacuated were still standing.

My own knowledge of St Kilda was very sketchy, and all I knew was that it was very remote and that the population had dwindled over the years until the few that were left had been evacuated to the mainland. We've always called the island Hiort in Gaelic, and my brother Donald, who had worked there, told me that although the English name was St Kilda, it was not actually named after a saint; in fact, there had never been a saint bearing that name. From Colin I learned that the Icelandic word *skildar*, meaning shields, had been the original name, probably a reference to the cliffs, and that over the years the name had been corrupted to become St Kilda. The Gaelic name of Hiort was also derived from the Icelandic language, from their word *hirtir* meaning deer; this was again a reference to the spiky peaks, which resembled deer's antlers when seen on the skyline.

Colin told me many interesting things about the island that had once been home to a thriving community and had its own parliament, where matters involving the inhabitants were decided. Although the island was effectively cut off from the rest of the world for eight months of the year, people had lived there for centuries, even before Roman times. At one time the population had numbered 200, but emigration and illness had gradually diminished their numbers, until in 1930, after a very bad winter, the last remaining residents decided to leave St Kilda for good.

I heard about the strange Soay sheep with their brown fleeces, the double-horned rams which still roamed the island like some exotic creatures from a far-off land and the cute brown mice that looked like small squirrels sitting up on their hind legs to eat nuts and seeds which they held in their front paws. They had no fear of the men in uniform who had come to share their island; instead, they would allow the soldiers to hand-feed them. The birds were many and varied, and they had once formed the mainstay of the indigenous population's diet. Their menfolk often scaled impossible-looking cliffs to catch gannets and fulmars, which they would store in *cleitean*, stone structures with turf roofs, against the hard days of winter. The St Kilda residents had left but the bird and plant life remained, and in 1956 the owner, the Marquis of Bute, had bequeathed the island to the National Trust for Scotland, who leased part of it to the Army. Most of the buildings used by the soldiers had been purpose-built, but the original factor's house was restored and used, and also the old Manse, which was refurbished and used as the Sergeants' Mess.

While on St Kilda, as telephone time was limited, Colin was allowed to make only two phone calls per week, each of twenty minutes' duration, and one evening he spent most of the time telling me about the haunted room in the old Manse where, by virtue of his rank, he now had his living quarters. When he had first arrived on the island he had been pleased to see that he had a room to himself — and then he found out why.

The room was at the end of the old Manse building next to the chapel wall; it was always extremely cold and there were hints from other soldiers of something other than mice appearing there at night. Someone told him not to look out of the window after dark, and he thought this was just a story made up by bored soldiers. Then one night he woke up and actually saw a black shape standing at the foot of the bed and he knew that this was no prank. The shape hovered for a while and disappeared into the air. Made of stern stuff, he continued to use that room and saw the otherworldly spectre on more than one occasion.

Once the numbers in the camp had risen, another soldier had to share his room, but he only stayed there for one night, as he too had seen the ghost and had sat up in bed white-faced and frozen with fear until morning. Then along came Dick, a Greek Cypriot sergeant who poohpoohed the whole idea and slept there soundly, night after night, with no visitations. So, after a night's drinking at the Puff Inn, a building designated for that purpose, Colin and his friends decided to puncture Dick's pompous rejection of the ghost theory. He had gone to bed early, and, as they could see that the light had gone out in the room, they knew that he was already asleep.

They went into the ruined chapel where they had seen the harp-like remains of an ancient piano and with great difficulty manoeuvred the large frame between them, trying to move quietly and frequently collapsing on top of it in fits of alcoholic giggles, until it was under Dick's window. They then proceeded to twang the old instrument and, choking with silent laughter, accompanied the ghostly music with eerie moans and groans. Although they kept this up for some time the light in the room stayed off and they thought that Dick had slept through it all. Much disgruntled, they took the frame back and went over to the Mess to drown their disappointment. There, in his pyjamas and as white as a sheet, stood Dick, a teetotaller, gulping a large brandy. He would not admit to having seen or heard anything.

Although he continued to sleep in the haunted room, he never referred to the ghost again, and when anyone tried to draw him out on the subject he went strangely quiet. When I heard that story I knew that my father's fears of my marrying a man who was too sensible for me were groundless.

The ghost may well have been the troubled spirit of a lady who had been banished to St Kilda by her husband before the '45 Rebellion and had been virtually imprisoned there for eight years. Her name was Lady Grange and her husband had been a strong supporter of the Jacobite cause; when the rebellion was being planned, she was caught eavesdropping on her husband and his plotting friends, so she was exiled to St Kilda lest she unwittingly pass on any incriminating information. Her husband had told everyone that she had died and even held a fake funeral for her, so she knew that she could never return home. She left St Kilda a few years before she died, but remained a prisoner right up until her death in 1745. I imagine that she must have been very unhappy with her situation and that her restless spirit could well be coming back to the scene of her imprisonment; however as there was no record of her ever having lived in the Manse, I can't imagine why she would choose to appear there.

Happily the half-term break at St Jude's coincided with Colin's return from St Kilda and, although I was in Uist for only a week, it was long enough for us to decide that, as his next posting could not be many months away, we would get married on Uist in the summer school holidays, regardless of whether I could get a job on the island or not. We would be leaving before long, so it was not important.

My parents were very pleased, especially my mother, who immediately began making long, long lists. The event was still six months away but she had waited a long time for this, as my elder brothers had got married on the mainland and she was raring to plan a wedding. Colin's family were also happy, as they very much wanted to come and see this strange place that they had been hearing about. The only fly in the ointment was that I was going to be stuck in Glasgow for much of the preparation time if something didn't change soon. So, as soon as I got back there I wrote a letter to J. A. MacLean, the Director of Education for Inverness-shire, explaining my situation, and awaited his answer without much hope.

I was stunned and delighted to receive his reply by return of post. My letter couldn't have come at a better time, he said. He had a school for me — the teacher was leaving unexpectedly for health reasons, and if I wanted it the school could be mine at Easter. I had specified that I would be leaving South Uist shortly after my marriage and would be available only for one term, but this suited him fine as he could appoint a new graduate for the autumn. If however, anything went wrong in my plans, I was welcome to talk to him again as and when. The formal contract was attached, and as he hadn't mentioned the school by name in his covering letter, I was apprehensive to say the least as I looked through all the legal stuff and found the name typed in. It was a small school in South Uist, South

Glendale Primary! And so I became the only teacher ever to be appointed to the little school by Glendale Bay twice. I was very pleased to accept the job.

The headmaster at St Jude's was sad but understanding, and the rest of my time in Glasgow was a blur of choosing a wedding dress, bridesmaids' dresses for my sister and my friend Mary, who was now engaged to Charles and was getting married a couple of weeks after me, and for the two little nieces, one from Colin's family and one from mine, who were also going to be bridesmaids. Mary's mother was beside herself with joy at having not only one bride-to-be but two to advise on all things pertaining to marriage, and I'm sure that James Dalzell breathed a sigh of relief when I said my goodbyes to them and left him with only one set of wedding plans ringing in his ears.

CHAPTER
TWELVE

"Is math an long a thug a-mach an cala às na dh'fhalbh i!" ("It's a good ship that returns to its port of departure!")

Neil Campbell greeted me with a proverb and one of his big grins as I parked PUS on Ludag jetty, above his boat.

"Jump in the boat," he said, "and save your feet for the wedding reel. I'll even take you twice around the bay if we have time. Just be careful or that big stone on your finger will sink the boat!"

It was good to be back, to see the hill looking lonely and peaceful in the spring sunshine. A few sheep stood out against the skyline, and no doubt behind its screening bulk the villagers of Glendale were busy with their morning chores. Neil had some stores for the school to deliver and had waited to give me a lift, so on my first day back for my brief return to the school where it had all begun, I didn't even have to walk the hill. I just had to sit back and listen to Neil and take in the beautiful clean, clear views of sea, islands and wheeling birds as we chugged our way around the headland and into Glendale Bay.

"I don't think you'll find many changes," Neil said. Then he added, "I think Eriskay has moved six inches to the right."

A welcome speech, engagement acknowledgement and a news update — all delivered "Neil style".

The old car PUS had been given a lot of attention by Colin when he was over from St Kilda; now that he had a car of his own, it was easier for him to come down to Kilpheder, and he had spent some time with my parents while I was away. He had given the car an overhaul and had also mended some of my father's implements that had been given up as beyond repair, including a small motorised tiller. Once the Major in charge of the workshops, a nasty bumptious little man, found him making a new part for the tiller and asked him which particular radar he was working on. When Colin told him what he was doing, the little Major got very angry about personal work being done in Army time. Colin reminded him that they had been instructed to "forge and maintain friendly relations with the native population". No more was said.

As the old car was working quite well, I no longer had to depend on the school bus and the spring weather made the hill walk pleasant, so I decided to live at home for the term that I would spend at Glendale School.

The car had always been considered as more of a family wagon than belonging to any specific member. My role in its purchase had been in partnership with Donald, and when repairs and other expenses were due whoever had the money to pay them picked up the bill.

Quite often my father did this, or if it was a simple job he would tackle it himself, so we all thought of it as our car and whoever needed it drove it. While I was in Glasgow my father had been using it to get to work until a few weeks before I came back, when the unthinkable happened — he lost his job.

I was not told anything about this until the evening of my return, but I knew that something was wrong as soon as I saw him. He bore the look of someone who had suffered a loss and was sad and angry at the same time. I had only seen this air about him once before, and that was when my brother Donald Angus had his accident. I knew that something bad had happened, but as I also knew that the family were all well I kept putting the thought to one side and hoping that my being home would make him forget whatever was troubling him. Unfortunately, it all went too deep for that.

In a nutshell, he and some other men from the factory had gone for a lunchtime drink at Polachar Inn, a regular Friday thing. On this Friday they were late back to work, and before they arrived back an Camshronach, the owner, had phoned from the mainland asking to speak to one of the absent men. The manager told him the situation and the owner asked if my father was with the absentees. When he was told that that was the case, he said, "When they come back, sack them all."

That was that.

On the following Monday morning all the other men went back to the factory, apologised and were given their jobs back. My father went to his grave convinced that it had been all been contrived to get rid of him. He was a staunch Labour supporter who never missed a chance of backing the owner, once his good friend, into a corner on matters political, and telling the other men how many good things the Labour MP had done for the island.

According to him, his employer had political aspirations of a more upper class orientation and was looking to the Western Isles for a seat. I don't know. I wasn't there at the time, and it was probably just his injured pride talking. It certainly seemed a bit severe to sack a senior staff member for coming back late on a Friday lunchtime — after all, a seaweed factory is hardly ICI — but I suppose he who pays the piper has the right to call the tune. I just saw the terrible things that taking away a man's dignity did to my father, and through him to his family. Of course he wouldn't go and beg to be reinstated, convinced as he was that it would only lead to further humiliation. Instead he went right off the rails. If he had been sacked for drinking, then he would live up to his newfound reputation, and the man we knew and had looked up to all our lives began to disappear.

The change didn't happen overnight, but gradually over a period of years he grew more and more bitter, and whereas before a glass of whisky only made him even better company, now it only brought a morose disillusioned person to the surface. Eventually reason prevailed and he gave up drinking altogether, but I don't think he ever quite recovered his self-respect.

Of course the aunties had a field day, but to give them their due, they confined their remarks to conversations with my mother and the rest of the family and did not openly antagonise my father. A wise decision, as his diplomacy of the past might not have checked his tongue in his current mood.

There was no occupational pension provided with the factory job and the staff was paid weekly, so he had been dismissed after a lifetime of working with smelly seaweed, and inhaling the white dust from the processed tangles, with one week's wages in his pocket. Knowing that there was little money in the pot, I said that I would pay all the wedding expenses myself, but the aunties rallied round and offered to pick up some of the bills as a wedding present. I had to grit my teeth and listen to a homily about idle drunken fathers losing their jobs and not being able to do their duty towards their children, but as it was going to cost them a pretty penny, I let them have their money's worth. I knew that my father had never been idle since his early years in Benbecula, when he had worked as a ploughboy even before he left school. The drinking was a result and not the cause of his present situation, but as I had been listening to their poor opinion of him since I was four and a half, it had all become like a boring record with the needle stuck. It would take more than their malicious carping to undermine my regard for him, so I just listened and accepted their offer with as much grace as I could muster.

At home, we all got used to hearing my father going over and over the "Why did he ask if I was with them before he gave the order?" question. It was best not to enter into any discussion on the subject and mostly we just left him to get on with it. Fortunately, getting it all off his chest seemed to help, and for the time I was with my parents in the run-up to the wedding there were no binges. My father promised me that he would do his best to look forward and not keep going back over things that troubled him, but it was very easy for me to give advice when I wasn't the person hurting. Once he told me: "It's very difficult, it is the last thing I think about every night when I close my eyes. First thing in the morning when I wake up and look at the clock to see how much time I have to do things around the house before I leave for work, it hits me. An Camshronach sacked me."

Poor man. There were many things to do round the croft and he spent much time tending the cows and mending fences. Although the number of cattle had dwindled over the years, there was still enough work to keep him busy and there was also the hay and corn to harvest. Money was tight, but it had been tighter in the old days, and thanks to my mother's ingenuity there was always plenty of food on the table.

My own mind had become very much taken up with thoughts of food, and how to prepare it. When I was a child my mother had taught me how to make a rabbit stew, as she couldn't bear to touch the creatures herself, so I cooked them for the family. I could open a tin of Spam and boil a mean potato, but that's as far as it went, and my coffee was acknowledged by all our family to be the worst in the world. The cookery lessons in Glasgow meant that I could make an edible curry and a hit-or-miss apple tart, but cooking anything else or even preparing a shopping list were skills that had passed me by. Little girls usually pick up that sort of knowledge when they are children, but I had not been encouraged to interfere in Auntie Chirsty's kitchen, and so in my early twenties I had to start learning at my mother's knee, as it were.

In her youth my mother had worked for a titled family in Oban, and as Mary the cook was a Uist girl my mother had spent a lot of her spare time in the kitchen, talking to her and being co-opted into helping with meal preparations. So she had a fund of tips to pass on to me and they saved my new husband from starvation when the time came. My father commented that it was a great pity that the rabbit population had been practically wiped out by myxomatosis, as I could have introduced Colin to my one and only foolproof recipe.

One thing I could never manage was a decent pancake. I don't mean the nice fat fluffy Scots pancakes that practically make themselves and walk off the griddle. I was fine with those. The ones that gave me so much grief were the thin English pancakes, or crêpes as they call them in France. Colin's mother could produce them by the basketful, mixing and stirring and tossing, with no trouble whatsoever. They were a total disaster for me. I spent many hours trying to produce a few for him when we were first married and after my first efforts I even had to throw the frying pan out. He says that he saw a seagull eating one of my discards and the

182

poor bird took five minutes to get off the ground. However, after a few lessons with my mother I could cook sufficient meals to keep body and soul together. Pancakes took a few more years.

Life at Glendale had indeed not changed a bit. The school roll had got even smaller and the actual teaching was more like giving a few nice children private tuition. Not like St Jude's at all. I had my lunch with Kate Ann and her mother every day and they were still the calm, sane people I had left. Although they had only met my father once when he and our neighbour John had gone over the hill to find a stray sheep on dipping day and had spent a few hours in their house before bringing the sheep back, they were full of concern for him and did their best to reassure me that his present state was just a passing phase. I drew comfort from them, as they had met adversity in their own lives and it had not destroyed them.

The MacIntyres were very excited about my forthcoming nuptials and couldn't get over how my plans had changed since leaving them.

"You were so determined to go to Canada. I thought you'd have been over there by now," Flora said, "but if it was meant to happen it would have happened."

They invited Colin out to tea, to see if "he was fit to walk the hill", as they put it, and they treated him like royalty. He thought that Glendale was a beautiful little place and really enjoyed meeting the people with whom I had spent so much time before I had met him. I only wished that old Calum had still been there — I would have liked to have heard them swapping fishing stories.

Colin loved to fish, especially if a boat was involved, and one day he and his friend Doug Braid, another Warrant Officer from the camp, had gone out from Loch Carnan pier to try and catch some of the big fish which they had heard about. They went right out into the Minch and started to use the feather line usually used for mackerel fishing. The result was spectacular — huge cod coming up three at a time. They caught so many that they were in danger of shipping water and had to stop. Colin brought his share of the catch straight down to Kilpheder, but as we had no deep freeze at the time he spent the evening going round the village dishing out free fish to all and sundry. I don't think he has ever had such a memorable day's fishing since then.

Doug Braid and his wife Barbara were old friends of Colin's and I was soon invited to meet them at their home in the married quarters of the camp at Balivanich. The house was one of the little Medway houses that had originally housed RAF officers many years ago. New officers' quarters had been built and the senior ranks were now quartered in the old Medways. The buildings didn't look like much from the outside, but inside they were surprisingly spacious and comfortable. All Army married quarters come complete with everything you and your family could possibly need, and this came as an agreeable surprise to me, as it cut out a lot of spending on furniture and other essentials. Meeting the Braids and other Army couples and hearing them reminisce about mutual friends and other places where they had all been together soon made me realise that an Army unit, at least at that time, was just like a large constantly moving family, and it allayed my secret fears about the life that would be mine before long.

My friendship with Jean went on as if the months in Glasgow hadn't happened. We saw each other often but now it was a different relationship. No more parties and dawn walks on the machair. Her father had died and she was very busy with the shop, which had been much extended. Her romance with John was going well and she too contemplated a departure from the island if it should lead to marriage. Her older brother and sister were the mainstay of the business and Jean, being much younger, was not quite as deeply interested in it as they were. John was coming to the end of his Army service and did not want to sign on for a further period, so there was some uncertainty about their future. It seemed that the previous year, when we had both been so carefree, belonged to two other girls. We were both very happy but our lives had become more serious. Dorothy was still in touch and was well content with her glamorous but tiring life as an air hostess, away from the dreaded "brats".

My father was pleased to know that I would be living in Benbecula, his old stamping ground, at least for a short time before leaving the island, and spent many evenings telling me stories about his own young days there. He had a deep love for the old Benbecula and, like most people who thought about it at all, he feared that the Army presence would change it forever. He could see the benefits but thought that they were going to cost Benbecula and especially Balivanich, much of its croft land and all of its character.

As always, he had a fund of information to pass on about the history of various places, like Culla Bay between Aird and Griminish, a beautiful curved inlet with the whitest of sands that he recommended for picnics in the summer. It was originally called Culla Mhoire ("Mary's Gift"), because of the legendary harvest of kelp brought in there by the tides. In the old days this was used by the people to fertilise their land and was also a source of income for the landlords.

I was intrigued by the name Columba Place which was given to a certain group of houses, and remarked that I hadn't heard of St Columba ever visiting Benbecula. He told me that there had also been a Loch Chaluim Cille ("Columba's Loch") in his young days but he thought he'd heard that it was being drained for some reason. On an island in the middle of the loch were the ruins of a little chapel called Teampall Chaluim Cille ("Columba's Temple"). It was all at least 1000 years old, he thought, and dated back to the time when one of the first monks who came to Balivanich arrived there from Ireland.

This monk had been driven out of Ireland and had asked God to lead him to a place where he could carry on his work. The tides and currents washed his little boat ashore on the coast of Benbecula and he started to build a chapel on the side of the loch. Every morning he would find that the stones had mysteriously moved out on to the island, so he deduced that he was meant to build the chapel there. When he finished his building he blessed the chapel and named it and the loch in honour of St Columba. Many monks came after him and that is how Balivanich got its name: Baile Mhanaich means "township of monks". It was a good story and it explained the Columba Place name, but I couldn't understand why God had wanted the chapel built on a tiny island in the middle of a loch. It didn't seem very congregation-friendly, but legends are always a bit puzzling.

It was good to see my father gradually getting back on form, and soon he was back to normal, doing concerts and even having a drink or two without becoming morbid. The first time he went on stage after the dismissal he did a kind of Dean Martin performance, staggering on to the stage and slurring his words, then tugging his forelock and saying: "Shorry, shir, work ish the cursh of the drinking clashes. I won't do it again . . . what do you mean? I won't get the shance, because you're shacking me?"

Following this with a few caustic but funny Gaelic references to his ex-employer got him over the embarrassment and back in with his audiences — they weren't to know how much it had cost him.

His teeth had always given my father a lot of trouble, and my mother, who had followed the old tradition of having all her lovely teeth out at the first sign of toothache, had no patience with his moans and groans.

"Off to the dentist with you and out with them all!"

In the end, after having had a few out but still having recurring problems with fillings, he decided to take her advice. In days gone by he would have had to wait until a dentist came to the island, but things had improved by this time and there was a nice young dentist living in Daliburgh, so the old situation of having to grin and bear it was no excuse. Reluctantly my father went over to the surgery to have an initial inspection, and the dentist agreed with my mother's diagnosis that a clean sweep would be the best thing.

An appointment was made and he settled down to wait. The very next day he had a letter from the BBC asking him to go to Glasgow to do a recording, on a date three days after he was due to have the teeth out. He really enjoyed the trips to Glasgow and by now knew most of the production team and his fellow artistes, so he decided to go, do the recording and leave the dental work until later. He got in touch with the dentist and tried to cancel his appointment, but as the dentist knew well how bad the teeth were, he was adamant. He had a packed book of appointments stretching far into the future, and if my father broke this one it could be a full six months before he could fit him in again. By that time, said the dentist, my father would not have to worry about his teeth any more: the gums would have become infected and he would be in Hallin cemetery, having died of blood poisoning. So my father capitulated. There were no earlier appointments that he could have, but the dentist asked him to come in for impressions straight away and said that he would have the dentures made up and ready to put in as the old teeth came out.

The much-feared day arrived and it all went smoothly. Dad was quite taken with his new teeth, giving the occasional grimace, but spending most of the time admiring his reflection in the mirror. The following day he was getting ready to catch the plane and he mentioned to my mother that the top set of dentures were very tight, as his gums were swollen, so she advised a salt and water mouthwash to ease the swelling. She made up a concoction for him and off he went to the bathroom to try it out.

With the top set taken out gingerly, he carefully rinsed his mouth out with the salt water, then spat into the lavatory pan and pulled the chain hard. As he took his hand away from the wooden handgrip at the end of the chain he knocked his dentures off the top of the cistern and straight into the gushing water. When our plumbing had been done by am Plumair Mòr (the big plumber) much talk had ensued about the desirability of having a very strong flushing system in your cisterns if you had no mains drainage for your sewage. Am Plumair Mòr had excelled himself by modifying our cistern so well that the flush, if pulled hard, could dispose of a half-grown cat. So my father's last sight of his new top set was brief as they rushed away towards the septic tank.

There was much lispy cursing from the direction of the bathroom, and we all waited for him to come in and tear up his plane ticket. Not so — he just took the bottom set out and carried on with his preparations. He didn't look too bad, as his gums were still quite swollen, but we wondered if he would be able to take part in the recording at all, with no teeth. When he came back from Glasgow he said that it hadn't been a problem. He'd spent the plane journey compiling a list of songs with maximum "Ho-ro"s and minimum "s" sounds and it all went very well. He gave us a demonstration before he changed out of his travelling clothes:

Hi horò, mo nighean donn,
Hi horì, mo nighean donn,
Hi horò, mo nighean donn a' chùil rèidh,
Mhaighdean òg a bha leam,
Bha do chomhradh rium ciùin,
Tha mo chridh' an-diugh trom na do dhéidh.

Hi horò, my brown maid,
Hi horì, my brown maid,
Hi horò, my brown maid flowing-haired,
Maiden young who with me
Kept such sweet company,
My poor heart is forlorn now you've gone.

We had to agree that he sounded just fine as long as you didn't look at his mouth.

"Good job it wasn't a TV recording," my mother said, conveniently forgetting that her advice had caused it all. If there is one thing on which my sister, brothers and I agree, it is that in an argument with my father, my mother never knew how to quit while she was ahead. Happily, on this occasion, as my father was flushed with the success of his trip, he just laughed and told us that he had been approached to take part in the first live TV broadcast of a new Gaelic programme

190

called 'Se 'ur Beatha ("You are Welcome") which was to take place in the near future and that he was going to see the dentist as soon as possible to make sure that he would be able to smile at the cameras.

The Glendale folk were getting all excited: men with tripods and measuring instruments had been seen on the hill and the consensus of opinion was that it must have something to do with the road. Their ongoing fight for a road had been a bone of contention for so long that they had given up believing that they would ever be able to step out of their houses and into a car. Of course, nobody told them what was going on, their letters went unanswered or got vague replies, and when one of them approached the engineers he was told that it was all just part of a survey. So that was that, again.

Kate Ann said: "They're waiting for us all to die and then they won't have to bother."

I must admit that, busy though I was with other things at the time, I wondered whether she might be right. It seemed such a shame. It was a really beautiful spot and the people had lived under such a disadvantage for so long, and with such good grace.

CHAPTER
THIRTEEN

I suppose it was only natural that the final days of my life as a single daughter of the croft should make me look around at the changes that had occurred in my surroundings since I had first become aware of them. The changes in my own family had been many, some good and some not so good. Most of the changes on the island, however, had been for the better.

Many of the innovations on the Uists taking place in the early days of the 1960s were probably as a result of the rising population and the granting of housing loans for crofters. Then there were more subsidies available than there had been in previous years, and although the croft could not yet be described, as I have seen in an article I read some time ago, as a "piece of land providing a good crop of subsidies and surrounded by a fence of regulations", things were going that way. A crofter could only have one dwelling place on his land and any usage of that land for purposes other than planting crops and raising cattle and sheep was very much frowned upon and needed so much unravelling of red tape that people didn't bother to try. The prices for cattle and sheep, although a lot better than today's derisory prices, were not good, and so making the land pay was difficult. Some crofts were just left idle as stock was run down to allow time for a day job. People visiting the island could easily think that the land should be put to some other use, but the crofter couldn't do anything about it as his hands were tied. Things have improved now and many crofters own their homes and land and some restrictions have been lifted, but not before time.

To begin with, the improvements were pretty much evenly spread over the Uists and Benbecula. However, over the years since the 1960s there has been a gradual shift in the pattern, with more and more emphasis on Benbecula, and Balivanich has become a kind of administrative capital. In my own opinion this is all very well as long as investment in other parts of the islands keeps pace and the development generated by Benbecula is spread out, and not merely drawn in and controlled there to cause economic sterility in other areas, as this would create an imbalance in the already frail social structure of the islands. However, this is all hindsight talking; in the early Sixties it still looked good.

The daily papers got to us a day after they had been on sale on the mainland, as they came on the afternoon plane, but you got used to reading "yesterday's news" if you lived on the island. There was no way round it and the shopkeepers could only give you the papers when they got them in themselves.

The shops we used then were the same ones as had been trading when I had gone to Daliburgh School as a pupil, the Co-op and A. C. MacDonald's, both much enlarged and carrying a much larger variety of stock. In Kilpheder we used to have a shop next door to our house run by the MacLellan family, but that had closed down and another small shop with a petrol station had been opened by Donald MacNeil out at Greybridge, on the Daliburgh-Kilpheder boundary, where there had been a shop many years ago. In addition, we had three travelling shops, the Co-op, A. C.'s and another from Boisdale owned by Finlay MacDonald, all of which came round on different days, so things had indeed improved.

The availability of a larger variety of foods brought about a change in our own family diet. In the old days we were never without a barrel of salt herring (one of my own all-time favourite meals with floury machair potatoes), which together with home-killed lamb and chicken provided our year-round sustenance. We bought beef and bacon from the shops, but more as a luxury than a necessity. Although I believe that pigs are now being kept on the island, in my young days they were not part of the crofter's stock. Perhaps the Hebridean soil was considered to be too soft for the rooting and wallowing in which a pig likes to indulge, so we never ate pork. My mother made our own butter and crowdie (cottage cheese) and also haggis and black puddings when an animal had been slaughtered. There had always been a vegetable patch on the croft where my father grew cabbage, turnips, carrots, beetroot and lettuce in season, so we were fairly self-sufficient. Now we had mince, pork chops and pies appearing on the table, and my father was introduced to tins of corned beef and spaghetti in a lurid orange sauce. Processed food had come to stay and the barrel of herring became a bucket and then disappeared altogether.

Quite a few people that I know of were diagnosed as diabetic in the years following this change. I have always wondered if there was any connection to the change in diet, as the condition had been unheard of in previous generations. Perhaps it was more a case that our doctors were better trained than before and that people may have been undiagnosed diabetics in the old days when our medical provision had been dire.

The healthcare situation had improved immensely by the 1960s. In addition to our dentist we had two excellent doctors in Daliburgh, Dr MacLean, who spoke fluent Gaelic and was very popular with the older folk, as they found it difficult to explain their aches and pains in English, and Dr Robertson, who combined the duties of GP and surgeon. The Robertson family were English-speaking but very nice and soon integrated into our community. They built a house near St Peter's Church and Mrs Robertson produced a beautiful rock garden there that was the envy of all who saw it. She and my father talked about flowers for hours, and after he'd been looking at her garden he'd say, "Now I'm going home to dig my garden up and throw it away."

My mother was actually a better gardener than he was, as he was used to planting things in rows, and clumps and clusters were foreign words to him. When Alick came home for a holiday, he was always trying to get new plants going, and then coming back to find that they'd been either dug up by my father, who hadn't recognised them, or been choked and overgrown because he was frightened to touch them, and had left them alone.

We still had many visitors to the house, and although an Camshronach no longer visited, Johnny Fincastle still dropped in from time to time. On the death of his father he had become the Earl of Dunmore, but apart from going a bit red in the face when he told us about it he didn't let his newly acquired exalted status make any difference to his enjoyment of my father's company. The last time I saw him he came to give me a lovely silver dish with a blue-glass lining as a wedding present, and every time I've used it I've thought what a genuinely nice young man he had been. He judged people by their character rather than their material worth and was a good ambassador for the aristocracy.

Rockets were being fired regularly from the rangehead on Iochdar machair and they generated a lot of interest locally. The rockets were unarmed Corporal missiles, and if you knew when the launching was taking place you could see them from the back of our house on a clear day. Sound travels very well in the clear Hebridean air, and we could hear a faint "boom" as the fuels ignited and sent the rocket high up in the sky before curving out over the Atlantic to be guided to its splashdown point. Nobody called them missiles; the word "rocket" made them sound so much less threatening and their firing was watched with curiosity, without anxiety.

One day, however, we saw what could happen if things went wrong, when one of the rockets went out of control for a few seconds and instead of following its prescribed trajectory turned round and headed back to land. The tracking team on the ground soon had the situation under control and it was blown up while still over the sea, but it made many people think of the consequences should this not have been the case. It did not carry a warhead but it could still have made a sizeable hole in the island had it exploded on land. The incident was soon forgotten and with our customary pragmatism we islanders concluded that the army knew what it was doing. There was a headline about it in one of the daily papers and my brother wrote a song about it, and that was that.

The man most violently opposed to the establishing of the range, Father John Morrison, had some years previously had a thirty-foot high statue of Our Lady of the Isles erected on the slopes of Rueval to celebrate the Marian Year. She stands with the baby in her arms looking out over Iochdar machair, and I think a lot of the older folk believed that as long as she was keeping an eye on Army activities all would be well. They were right on that particular day at least.

My own Army activities had been curtailed slightly in the run-up to the wedding when Colin was sent over to St Kilda yet again. As he was leaving his car with me for the three-week period of his absence, I drove him to Loch Carnan pier, where he and other soldiers boarded a dreadful old boat called *The Mull* for eight hours of heaving and rolling through seas that were never calm. The passage itself was always difficult, but docking at Village Bay on the island was the real test of mettle.

The island of St Kilda lies in a high wind corridor and at high tide the bay resembles a boiling cauldron if the wind blows from the east. *The Mull* anchored in the bay and the soldiers were ferried ashore in a little dory. From the heaving little wooden boat they had to jump on to a pitching raft made from planks and car tyres and attached to the pier by ropes, then climb up on to the jetty. As the raft could only be floated at high tide, nobody could predict whether actual arrival on the island would take minutes, hours or be abandoned if the wind was too high. Knowing about this made my own hillwalking seem pretty tame. However, like my fellow islanders I was confident that the army knew what it was doing, so I didn't worry too much about it, as the forthcoming wedding took up most of my thinking time.

I learned much about weddings in the run-up to my own, and I think one of the things which surprised me most was that a lot of the preparations have nothing at all to do with the actual wedding. How could painting the outside of our house be classed as a wedding preparation? I must admit that I left my parents to do what they liked, as it seemed to keep them happy. The lists were made up and lost and made up again, and I have a sneaking suspicion that when it came to making the final plans and sending out invitations, my mother never actually consulted any of her bits of paper. My own list was short: 3 July — wear white dress, go to St Peter's, get married.

As the day approached I was given a lot of advice about what not to do on my wedding day, and one little hint has stuck in my mind: do not put your wedding dress on over a pair of trousers. A cousin of mine gave me this gem of wisdom based on her own experience. On her wedding morning she'd made all the usual preparations and had a bit of time in hand, so rather than put her wedding dress on too early she had dressed in a pair of navy trousers and a top. Time had gone on and when the car arrived to take her to church she still hadn't changed, so the dress and veil were put on in a rush. As she walked up the aisle she felt something falling around her ankles, and when she looked down she could see the navy trousers bunching out from under the hem of her white satin dress. She thought that she'd taken them off, but in the rush to get dressed she had only unzipped them. There was a short pause in her progress towards the altar, while she stepped out of the trousers and kicked them under a seat.

During the twice-weekly, twenty-minute phone calls from St Kilda, much of the time was spent talking about things pertaining to the wedding, but I was interested to hear that the "Ghostbusters" were at it again. Scattered about the island was the wreckage of several planes that had crashed on St Kilda during the war years, and this had aroused much interest and curiosity in the minds of the khaki-clad incomers. They decided to hold a kind of séance with an Ouija board to try and contact the spirits of the aircrews. The séances got going late at night, usually in conjunction with the intake of liquid spirits, and appeared to be very successful; they soon established contact with the crew of one aircraft, and got all their names, ranks and numbers and the type of aircraft that they had been flying. They also gleaned the information that one crew member had survived for two weeks before dying of his terrible injuries. As all this appeared to be an important new revelation, Colin took it upon himself to inform the Air Ministry of the facts. After some time he had a reply. It had been all rubbish — no such plane, no such people. "Stop wasting Air Ministry time or we'll inform your Commanding Officer," the letter said. I am relieved to say that that was the last time he dabbled in the occult.

By the time he returned from St Kilda I had some exciting news for him: the Glendale road had been approved and work would be starting any day. I don't know if all the letters written by various people had been a trigger in any way at all, but at least now the little community living round the bay could have a better life and they were all looking forward to the day when the road would finally be opened. There was a bit of poetic justice meted out by the Council, who had been bombarded with letters from generations of Glendale teachers — the first thing they did after the road was opened was to close the school. I suppose it made economic sense to bus the few children there to a larger school, but that little building had been so much more than an educational establishment. It had been a symbol of contact with the outside world and over the years had provided valuable service to the community. It had been a school, chapel, meeting-place and focal point among the scattered dwellings. Still, I suppose losing it was a small price to pay for gaining the road.

Our wedding presents were arriving and beginning to take over the house. In fact one of them was grazing away on Tobht' 'IcIlleChriòsda ("Gilchrist's Ruin"), the hillock behind our house. One of the Glendale families had given me a beautiful tray made of rosewood and inlaid with butterfly wings, which I had seen and admired when their son came home from sea, and they had also presented me with a sheep. The wedding was going to be the traditional type with all the catering and cooking done by the bride's family, but some of the meat (mainly chicken) and other goods were supplied by the guests, and the sheep was meant to be slaughtered and roasted for this purpose. However, I had strong feelings about eating anything which had been baa-ing a "good morning" to me each day, and it remained on our croft in happy retirement, at least until I was safely off the island. I think it eventually found its way to my parents' table, as I remember my father giving us the fleece to use as a bedside rug some years later.

Any bride-to-be can tell you that in the weeks preceding her wedding someone seems to press a fast-forward button and there's never enough time to do the things that need to be done. So it was for me, and in no time at all I was laden with presents walking back over the hill for the last time. I would love to be able to say that I took a last long look at the houses and the bay, but in reality I just scuttled along as fast as I could, as I was already late for something which at the time seemed more important. I should have taken that last look, because the next time I went out to Glendale, some years into the future, the school was gone, many of the old houses had been replaced and very few of the old people remained to admire the wide black ribbon of road along which I was driving.

Many of the wedding guests were coming over from the mainland and a party of new in-laws was also expected, so there was much to plan. Some people were spending a few days at our house and others were to be accommodated at the houses of friends. Here comes another tip about weddings: always keep your bridesmaids under the same roof on the night before the wedding. I didn't, and someone forgot to send a car for one of the small bridesmaids — it would have to be the little English niece — who had to run all the way to the church in her pretty little dress and brocade shoes. Fortunately, the house where she was sleeping wasn't too far away from St Peter's but it couldn't have given her much of a good impression of us, especially as she had been made to eat real oatmeal porridge for the first time that morning.

My friend Mary from Glasgow had volunteered to bring the wedding dress with her, as I had so much luggage to bring with me when I returned to the island. It was quite an elaborate dress, with a bustle, train and two hooped petticoats, and the last time I had seen it hanging on its satin hanger it didn't seem like too large a transportation problem. Poor Mary — when I saw her coming off the ferry with a box resembling a large coffin I knew that I should have made other arrangements. Fortunately for our continuing friendship, her fellow-passengers had given her some help.

July was a very popular month for island weddings, as the weather is usually nice at that time, so on the day that my future in-laws travelled on the *Claymore* a lot of the passengers were coming to the island for some wedding or other. I've heard them talking about it afterwards and saying, "Everyone on that ferry was going to the wedding."

They are friendly folk and had really enjoyed talking to all and sundry on the boat, but in much the same way as you'll get asked in America whether you know the Smiths who live in London, they assumed that because they were going to an island everybody knew everyone else. Even in those days that was not strictly true. However, they had been to Edinburgh and had travelled through the beautiful Highlands on their way to Uist and thought that Scotland was awesome, so I didn't really mind the fact that on their arrival in Kilpheder they appeared to be rather surprised that I actually lived in a house and not in a bothy.

My mother had gone to Glasgow to buy outfits for herself and the aunties and had returned with very blue hair. She had been advised by her friends to have a blue rinse on her white hair and something had gone wrong. It was very startling. Fortunately it was the type of product that mellowed with age, and after a few shampoos she was shouting, "For God's sake don't wash it all out, I paid good money for this!"

Her outfit was very nice, but as we lined up to receive the guests on my wedding morning, I couldn't help noticing that the dress and jacket that my new mother-in-law, a skilled dressmaker, had made for herself was almost identical, both in colour and style. Still, the hats were different. Colin and my father were exempt from all this feminine preoccupation with appearance. My father flatly refused to buy a new suit, as he insisted that his current best suit had only just been broken in, and Colin was getting married in dress uniform.

The wedding ceremony was to be held in St Peter's Church, the old building in which I had been christened and which had dominated our landscape since the mid-1800s, and as I had a history of fainting when kneeling upright, discovered in my convent days, Monsignor MacKellaig told me that he'd have the velvet chairs placed as close to the kneelers as possible. I think that was just about the full extent of my input to the actual planning of the day.

After the ceremony the bride and groom were to head a procession, led by two pipers, across the road to the church hall, where the reception would be held. The greeting of guests would take place at the inside door of the hall, and the whole of the floor would be filled with dining tables for the wedding lunch which would form the first part of the reception. Then would come speeches and the reading of greetings telegrams and a short interval during which the floor would be cleared for dancing. Tables set up on the stage would take care of remaining guests and latecomers, and the waitresses would carry on serving the lunch meal until about five o'clock, when the menu would change to a high tea, also served on the stage. Whisky and sherry were to be provided at the table for toasts, and beer would be on tap from barrels set up in the back room. This had been the format for weddings at St Peter's since the hall had first been opened, so the wedding really organised itself.

After the clearing of the hall, tradition decreed that the bride and groom led off the dancing with the Bridal Reel, but here we decided to have a slight alteration, due to the nationality of my bridegroom. He was game for anything, but I did not want him to give the assembled guests the pleasure of watching him give the usual Sassenach's version of Scots Reel steps: hopping on one foot, kicking the other in the air and shouting "Whee!" — mean of me, I know, so we opted for a waltz instead. This was a first, and I believe it caused talk: "Could she be hiding something under the hoops?"

Time gave the lie to that one, but my mother also told me that some people were annoyed that we left the reception before it ended. We had to do this so that we could catch the only plane that week which would make the connection to our onward flight to Norway, where we'd booked our honeymoon. It was a long time ago, but if anybody still feels offended, sorry, folks.

If it's any consolation, I was less than pleased to find that our plans for a discreet departure from the island had been scuppered by whoever arranged for two pipers in full Highland Dress to meet us at Balivanich Airport and pipe us aboard the plane to the strains of "Highland Wedding", prompting the Captain to welcome us aboard and wish us a long and happy life together. No doubt whoever did it meant well, but it was very embarrassing as we were stared at for the whole duration of the flight.

We had chosen Norway for our honeymoon, as Colin had visited it briefly before and wanted to see more of it. I had always wanted to see the country that had once been bound to my own island, with its fjords and glaciers. The country was lovely and the people generally very hospitable, even if my brand new wedding ring went unnoticed, as the married women of Norway wear their rings on their right hands.

My wedding day, like those of most brides I've spoken to, went by in a kind of blur. Several little things have stuck in my mind, however, like the *Daily Express* reporter who kept making a thorough nuisance of himself: incensed at being banned from taking photographs inside the church, he gave Colin the headline "Rocketing Cupid" and published a picture in which the groom had his eyes shut and the bride looked as if she was gearing up to have a good spit.

I remember seeing Colin standing with his brother Ken by the altar and thinking "My goodness, he looks white. I hope his seat is close to the kneeler."

My friend Jean was driving the wedding car and I can remember thinking that she was much more nervous than I was, stepping on my dress at least twice as she helped me out of the car. I remember her saying, "Isn't this better than Canada?"

Strange the ironies of life. Both she and Dorothy, the two people who had been so much against my going there, settled in Canada themselves after they were married, and although I've had homes on three different continents over the years, it took me twenty-five years to visit Canada. Beautiful land! I have been back many times for visits and I know that, contented as I have been, had my world taken a different spin I would have found it hard to come home at the end of the intended two years.

Clearest of all my memories is that of my wedding morning, waiting for the car to arrive in a house strangely quiet and empty of people, with nobody left but my father, who, uncharacteristically, was rehearsing his wedding speech. Earlier he had told me that although I was now going to "belong" to someone else, I would always be his daughter. He was not given to emotional speeches but I knew what he meant, and I think he also knew that I have never "belonged" to anyone but myself since the age of four and a half and never would. Belong with, certainly, but not belong to. If the truth were known he had always remained his own person too — *am Badhlach*, the Benbecula man, as some South Uist people still called him after a lifetime of living in Kilpheder. The man waiting for me at the church had needed to be self-sufficient all his adult life too, as his father had deserted the family when he was just fourteen.

So, as I stood in my room, at the window that looks directly on to the old house, my thoughts were not concerned with the future: I was confident that it was in safe hands. Instead, my eyes were filled with scenes from the past engendered by the sight of that old building with the sagging thatched roof. They were filled with memories of Hallowe'ens and Hogmanays, of long-gone people like Mary by the Canal and her old "bad dog". I could almost hear my mother and Donald Angus holding their music competitions before his accident had put paid to his musical achievements, and smiled as I heard again the shout of "Goal!" on the night of the dumpling. I felt once more the feeling of warmth and security that had surrounded me when I stepped through the crofthouse door on the night that I had run away from Barra to attend my very first island wedding. Memories of childhood and young adulthood all centred round the sustaining constant of the little crofthouse and its occupants — memories that would never fade. By the time Jean arrived with the car to take me to my own island wedding, I was calmer than my father, who was still muttering his lines, and I knew that I was not saying goodbye to anything at all, and that whatever the future might bring I could always come back — back to the croft, back to the family, and back to the island.

Also available in ISIS Large Print:

Branching Out

Rod Broome

"Perched nervously on the edge of the settee, I declared my love for his daughter, laid out my future prospects, and assured him of my intention to treat her well. I think he felt as awkward as I did, and quickly gave his consent."

After finishing his National Service, Rod Broome began Teacher Training in Didsbury. Although hard work, life at college was enjoyable and he shares many tales from the Social Room and his "Brew Club". And it was at college that he met his future wife, Anita.

We follow Rod through his early days as a teacher, and his experiences with pupils and other staff. He also talks about his blossoming romance and life as a courting couple, through to the early days of their marriage and their first home.

ISBN 978-0-7531-9500-0 (hb)
ISBN 978-0-7531-9501-7 (pb)

Hellfire and Herring

Christopher Rush

"You could smell God on the air in St Monans as surely as you could smell herring."

Hellfire and Herring is a vivid, powerful and moving account of Christopher Rush's upbringing in the 1940s and 1950s in St Monans, a small fishing village on the east coast of Scotland.

In an evocation of a way of life now vanished, Rush weaves stories from the fabric of family life, village characters, church and school. He writes of folklore and fishing, the eternal power of the sea and the cycle of the seasons. He also reflects on the relationship with his parents, and the inescapability of childhood influences far into adult life.

ISBN 978-0-7531-9506-2 (hb)
ISBN 978-0-7531-9507-9 (pb)

The Tartan Pimpernel

Donald Caskie

"I had caught up with a struggling mass of people when German and Italian aircraft streaked down from the sky. Machine guns spat indiscriminate death. Bombs thudded and exploded all along the road."

This is the remarkable story of Donald Caskie, minister of the Scots Kirk in Paris at the time of the German invasion of France in 1940. Although he had several opportunities to flee, Caskie stayed behind to help establish a network of safe houses and escape routes for Allied soldiers and airmen trapped in occupied territory. This was dangerous work, and despite the constant threat of capture and execution, Caskie showed enormous resourcefulness and courage as he aided thousands of servicemen to freedom.

Finally arrested and interrogated, he was sentenced to death at a Nazi show trial, and it was only through the intervention of a German pastor that his life was saved.

ISBN 978-0-7531-9496-6 (hb)
ISBN 978-0-7531-9497-3 (pb)

The Flight of the Young Sparrow

Trudi Spatz

"No one spoke a word as we all had our own thoughts about the unknown future. Kurt and I looked out of the window, a last glance of Hamburg, and we wondered whether we would ever see Hamburg again."

This is the fascinating account of the experiences of Trudi Spatz in the turbulent years before, during and after the Second World War. Brought up as a young girl in Nazi Germany, she and her family managed to escape to England in 1938 after her father fell foul of the authorities. Her memoir charts the family's struggle for survival and the many trials and tribulations they faced whilst trying to live as "free" citizens in wartime England.

Eventually, Trudi was called up for service and embarked on a new phase in her life. She found herself undertaking a series of varied jobs, eventually reaching her longed-for goal — to become a teacher.

ISBN 978-0-7531-9488-1 (hb)
ISBN 978-0-7531-9489-8 (pb)

The Grocer's Granddaughter

Rose Parish

"The English are often referred to as 'A Nation of Shopkeepers', and my family were certainly among them."

As the child of a family running a busy village shop, the author developed the ability to be "a fly on the wall" watching, listening and establishing lasting memories. She has drawn up a very special picture of life in the Worcestershire village of Ombersley during the 1940s. This is a pithy account of village life as it was, offering a view decidedly unlike a picture-postcard image. The full stratum of village life is reflected, drawing attention to a variety of ideas and attitudes; poverty, wealth, a common work ethic, crime, tragedy, sorrow and pleasure are all there in the village mixing pot.

ISBN 978-0-7531-9482-9 (hb)
ISBN 978-0-7531-9483-6 (pb)

ISIS publish a wide range of books in large print, from fiction to biography. Any suggestions for books you would like to see in large print or audio are always welcome. Please send to the Editorial Department at:

ISIS Publishing Limited
7 Centremead
Osney Mead
Oxford OX2 0ES

A full list of titles is available free of charge from:

Ulverscroft Large Print Books Limited

(UK)
The Green
Bradgate Road, Anstey
Leicester LE7 7FU
Tel: (0116) 236 4325

(Australia)
P.O. Box 314
St Leonards
NSW 1590
Tel: (02) 9436 2622

(USA)
P.O. Box 1230
West Seneca
N.Y. 14224-1230
Tel: (716) 674 4270

(Canada)
P.O. Box 80038
Burlington
Ontario L7L 6B1
Tel: (905) 637 8734

(New Zealand)
P.O. Box 456
Feilding
Tel: (06) 323 6828

Details of **ISIS** complete and unabridged audio books are also available from these offices. Alternatively, contact your local library for details of their collection of **ISIS** large print and unabridged audio books.